my favourite
cheap eats

Calgary, Banff and beyond
2nd edition

John Gilchrist
edited by Catherine Caldwell

Escurial Incorporated
Calgary, Alberta

Published by
Escurial Incorporated
9519 Assiniboine Road SE
Calgary, Alberta
Canada T2J 0Z5
Phone: 403.255.7560
Email: escurial@telus.net

Library and Archives Canada Cataloguing in Publication

Gilchrist, John, 1953–
    My favourite cheap eats : Calgary, Banff and beyond / John Gilchrist ; edited by Catherine Caldwell. —2nd ed.

    Includes index.
    Issued also in electronic format.

    ISBN: 978–0–9868584–0–6

    1. Restaurants—Alberta—Calgary Region—Guidebooks.   2. Calgary Region (Alta.)—Guidebooks.   I. Caldwell, Catherine, 1956–   II. Title.

TX907.5.C22A43   2011   647.957123'38   C2011–903029–2

Credits:
Interior Design: Jeremy Drought, Last Impression Publishing Service,
    Calgary, Alberta
Cover Design: Pierre Lamielle, Calgary, Alberta
Printed and bound in Canada by Marquis Book Printing Inc., Montreal,
    Quebec

Contents

Acknowledgements

THIS being my ninth book, I've had the opportunity to work with many talented people on an ongoing basis. This page is where I get to thank them.

There's Jeremy Drought who handles the interior design of the book. That means he creates a readable page and sets everything up so the printer can deal easily with it—no mean feat. He can talk about fonts and kerning and leading with the best of them (which definitely doesn't include me!).

There's Pierre Lamielle, too, who came up with a pair of salt and pepper shakers to show that this is the 2nd edition of *Cheap Eats*. Brilliant and simple. Why can't I think like that?

And I have to thank Brenda and Richard White, whose timely comments always help us see the obvious.

I am most thankful for the work of the tenacious Catherine, my editor and wife of many years. And let me just mention here that she's the reigning World Porridge Making Champion in the Specialty Section (Scotland, October 2010) and feeds me more steel-cut oats than any horse has ever eaten. Without her talents, my culinary ramblings would never be palatable to the eye. And my cholesterol wouldn't be so low.

Introduction

WELCOME to a big second helping of *My Favourite Cheap Eats*. This is a compilation of places I visit in Calgary, Banff and other spots in Southern Alberta when I want breakfast or lunch for under $15 or dinner for under $20. Over half of the eateries here are new to this edition, but I've revisited and included many old favourites as well.

The first edition of *My Favourite Cheap Eats* was a great pleasure to write and was fortunately well received. That was three years ago, and the positive reception probably had something to do with the book's launch coinciding with the arrival of the recession.

Now, with the recession waning but still in the memories of both diners and restaurateurs, we've seen a change in the way we eat out. Many of the bloated, over-the-top restaurants of the boom period have either disappeared or turned their attention towards value to go along with quality and creativity. Same with a lot of the contemporary restaurants that have opened since the recession hit—they're starting out leaner, smaller and more focused than their predecessors used to, and they've been put together on tight budgets. But they're still very professional and pushing the cutting edge of contemporary cuisine. Many of these new, hot places are priced beyond this book's budget (that's OK—we want choices), but some have made it in because they're not.

The focus on value has also kept—and perhaps increased—our attention on the multicultural aspect of Calgary and area. We're interested in a globeful of flavours, and of course, if we can get it for cheap, all the better. So you'll see places in this book that serve Nepalese, Neapolitan, Ukrainian, Jamaican, Mexican and even Québécois cuisine. And one trend I've noticed is a huge growth in Vietnamese, Middle Eastern, and Indian and Pakistani restaurants.

What else? I see lots of coffee shops getting seriously into food, ensuring they have business after the morning caffeine rush. Plus, there are a lot more breakfast places and diners around now. And finally—believe me when I tell you that gardens of coleslaw are cropping up. I ate a ton of it in the research for this book. Which makes sense—coleslaw is a great recession food.

But now, let's get into the nitty-gritty of *Cheap Eats*:

- As I mentioned above, restaurants reviewed in this book serve breakfast or lunch for under $15 or dinner for under $20. You can always break that budget, so choose your dishes carefully.

- Entries are arranged (mostly) alphabetically. Near the end of the book, however, there are a few pages of what I call the "More" entries, and these unfortunately break that nice alphabetical order—I wanted to bring a few extra treats to your table.

- All entries appear at least twice in "The Lists" index at the back.

- Hours are always subject to change. So call ahead.

- In the sidebars, abbreviations under "Cards" are as follows: **V** for Visa, **MC** for MasterCard and **AE** for American Express. If a place has an Automated Teller Machine available, I've included **ATM** to indicate so in this category.

- In the sidebars under the "Drinks" heading, I have indicated whether or not licensed establishments offer corkage. Corkage means you can bring your own unopened bottle of wine to the restaurant to be opened and served there, and I have also indicated the cost of that service if it exists.

- Under the "Takeout" category in the sidebars, I've included "Delivery" if that option is available. Be aware, though, that delivery has its limits. A place that delivers in Canmore may be reluctant to drive to your home in, say, Turner Valley.

- I've included Facebook and/or Twitter logos for establishments that have a presence on those social media.

So enjoy. Thank goodness we still consume food one bite at a time—no Jetsons' food pills yet. There's still a lot of great—and cheap—food out there. And it's not just coleslaw.

John Gilchrist
Calgary, Alberta

Aida's | Lebanese

I**T** seems I can't write a book without including Aida's. Aida's (the restaurant) and Aida (the person) have been near the top of my list since this place opened in 2000. The restaurant has fine Lebanese food, good prices and a warm, friendly (and usually crowded) setting, too. A smiling hello from Aida or her staff always makes me feel good.

But let's look closer at the food. The fattoush is one of my favourites here, regardless of the jokes I've made over the years about the sound of the word. The crunchy romaine, fresh tomatoes, green peppers, radishes, onion and pita chips doused in an olive oil and sumac dressing are so good.

Then there's the mouhammara—the red-pepper, pomegranate juice and walnut dip. It beats hummus—and I really like her hummus—all to heck.

And how about her kibbeh, the football-shaped ground beef and cracked-wheat shells filled with more beef and almonds and served with a mint-yogurt dip? Not only are they tasty, but they seem impossible to make. I've tried on a couple of occasions and can't do it, so I just leave it to Aida.

Let's not forget her falafel either or her chicken shawarma, her kafta kebab and all the other great dishes on her menu. So until further notice, it looks like Aida's will continue to be in my books.

Address
2208 – 4 Street SW

Phone
403.541.1189

Hours
Monday
11 am – 9 pm

Tuesday – Thursday
11 am – 10 pm

Friday & Saturday
11 am – 10:30 pm

Reservations
Highly recommended, especially weekends

Cards
V, MC, AE, Debit

Drinks
Fully licensed
No corkage

Takeout
Yes

Outdoor Dining
No

Website
aidasbistro.ca

Air Side Bistro

Casual Continental

AIR Side Bistro in the Landmark Aviation Centre is one for the aeronautical fan. It has a great location, facing as it does onto the main runway of Calgary International Airport. It's been a favourite spot for years—in various restaurant identities—because of its full-length windows that showcase private jets and big commercial planes departing from and landing at YYC.

Air Side's customers are an eclectic bunch: oil execs hopping a corporate jet to the oilfields, military folks waiting for flights to training grounds, nearby office workers needing a tasty lunch and just plain old airplane fans. Some want the window seats, others couldn't care less.

But aside from being a place to while away a lunch hour, dreaming of faraway destinations and perhaps ogling performers or sports teams passing through, Air Side offers a comfortable menu of sandwiches like beef dips and meatball paninis, salads like Cobbs and Caesars with cured salmon, and hot entrees like turkey meat loaf and lentil moussaka. It's skilfully prepared food, perfect for a noon hour of plane-watching. And it's priced well, with most items under $12.

The look of Air Side hasn't changed much over the past couple of decades. It has the feel of an airport departure lounge—which it partly is—and furniture that dates it to the 1980s. Which is not necessarily a bad thing because it's all in good shape. It reminds me of a time when air travel was more casual and comfortable than it's become lately.

Address
1441 Aviation Park NE
(Landmark Aviation Centre)

Phone
403.295.4140

Hours
Monday – Friday
7 am – 3 pm

Sunday
10 am – 2 pm

Reservations
Recommended

Cards
V, MC, AE, Debit

Drinks
Fully licensed
No corkage

Takeout
Yes

Outdoor Dining
No

Website
airsidebistro.com

Alberta King of Subs

Smoked Meat

WHILE the debate over where to find a good Montreal smoked meat sandwich in Calgary continues unabated, many aficianados of the genre have declared their allegiance to Alberta King of Subs. And certainly, it will be on almost anyone's short list.

Not for the decor, though, unless you think that smoked meat shows best when lit by fluorescents and surrounded by aging plastic. So AKS isn't much to look at, but they sure do slice a fine sandwich.

In true Montreal style, too, with imported (from Quebec) smoked meat steamed and hand-cut onto local rye bread (mustard, optional) and served in sizes ranging from merely large to outrageously humongous. Add a side of home-cut fries—deliciously poutined if you'd like—and a kosher dill, and maybe throw in a spruce beer or a Labatt 50. While it may not be Schwartz's Deli in La Belle Ville, the fare is a reasonable facsimile.

The staff take their jobs seriously here. They understand that smoked meat fans are hard to please, so they do their best to make them happy. The food arrives hot and fast and with the confidence that it will be appreciated.

If you peruse the menu (regulars don't), you'll notice that AKS offers a range of both cold and grilled subs and even hamburgers and steamed or grilled hot dogs. I'm sure they're all great, but I've never seen anyone ever order them. At AKS, smoked meat reigns.

Address
7196 Temple Drive NE

Phone
403.293.5809

Hours
Monday – Wednesday
10 am – 9 pm

Thursday – Saturday
10 am – 10 pm

Sunday
11 am – 9 pm

Reservations
Not accepted

Cards
V, MC, Debit

Drinks
Beer & coolers only
No corkage

Takeout
Yes
Delivery

Outdoor Dining
No

Website
albertakingofsubs.com

Babylon

Middle Eastern

A VISION of the ancient Hanging Gardens of Babylon comes to mind when I open the door at this Babylon. Not that the place is floral—rather, it's the sight and scent of shawarma and donair spinning on spits like whirling dervishes, the pots of meats and vegetables glowing under heat lamps and the colourful pictures of all the dishes hanging overhead that create a hyper-stimulated aura.

But I maintain my calm, and I focus on the task at hand—lunch. The house-made chicken shawarma, a stack of boneless, skin-on chicken breasts slowly sizzling on the spit, is tempting. And those pots of steaming meats and vegetables are attractive, simmering in a rainbow of sauces. They're stews of sorts—there are no labels on them so I'm not positive what they are. I've had a few of them before, though, so I'm sure they would taste great.

What I'm really here for is the house-made lamb donair in a pita with pickles, fresh vegetables and sauces, both sweet and garlicky. Slices of the lamb donair are first tossed on the grill for heating. (The meat has been pre-cooked, pre-sliced and chilled for just such a moment.) Then the slices are laid onto the pita, topped with my own selection of pickles, veggies and sauces, and rolled up. For $8.39, I've got a primo lunch to-go.

Or, if you want, you can choose to dine in at one of Babylon's thirty-five seats. Without a plant in sight.

Address
255 – 28 Street SE
(Short Pants Plaza)

Phone
403.272.2233

Hours
Monday – Saturday
9 am – 7 pm

Reservations
Not accepted

Cards
V, MC, Debit

Drinks
No alcoholic beverages

Takeout
Yes

Outdoor Dining
No

Website
No

Banh Mi Thi Thi

Vietnamese Subs

TALK to fans of banh mi (Vietnamese baguette sandwiches) and a couple of names pop up. The estimable Trung Nguyen, reviewed elsewhere in this book, is one. And Banh Mi Thi Thi is the other. There are many banh mi outlets around, but these two are the ones that do the sandwiches best. And they are just around the corner from each other.

Banh Mi Thi Thi is hidden in a building that faces 1st Street SE, across from the Harry Hays Building and quite near the river. Parking is near-impossible in this area. But if you've got someone with you, pull into the loading zone out front and, just in case, leave your friend the car keys while you dash in to order. (Bring cash!)

There wouldn't be enough room for both of you inside the cafe anyway. Well, maybe. The ordering section of Banh Mi Thi Thi is tiny; the kitchen, not much bigger. Two people in the kitchen, two out front and it's more than full.

Order up a peppered beef or lemon-grass chicken sandwich, choose your toppings—lettuce, tomato, cilantro, onion, pickled carrots, chilies—and you'll have a primo sandwich to-go in loading-zone seconds. Careful with the chilies. One tiny red beggar, looking hot enough to explode, will be more than enough for most people.

Then hop back in the car with your prizes. Next question: Where to go to chow down?

Address
209 – 1 Street SE

Phone
403.265.5452

Hours
Monday – Friday
10:30 am – 6 pm

Saturday
10:30 am – 5 pm

Reservations
Not accepted
(No seating)

Cards
Cash only

Drinks
No alcoholic beverages

Takeout
Yes

Outdoor Dining
No

Website
No

Barpa Bill's

Greek

BARPA Bill's has consumed a small corner of Banff's Bear Street since 1997, becoming a must-visit for many on their trips to the Rockies. It's tiny, with only a dozen or so stools, and it's tucked into an ordinary-looking building. But you won't need a GPS unit to find it. Unless your GPS is a "Garlic Positioning System," that is. Stroll anywhere near Bear Street and you'll likely pick up a waft of the Greek kitchen, the intermingling of grilled lamb, garlic, olive oil and tzatziki. Heavy on the garlic.

The menu is simple—lamb souvlaki, chicken donair, Greek and Caesar salads, spanakopita (spinach and feta in phyllo), dolmades (grape leaves stuffed with rice), hummus and baklava are pretty much the options. The sauce of choice is the garlicky tzatziki, and the condiments include tomato, cucumber, onion and lettuce. Load up your souvlaki and you'll have a culinary epiphany that will tingle your tonsils for hours.

But if you want an East-meets-West experience, chuff back a beef burger or Bill's new lamb burger. Also topped with aromatic sauces, these babies will help transport you to a good Greek place before long.

To continue your Aegean sojourn, pull up a stool, gaze into the framed photos of the Greek isles and listen to Bill and his wife Janna tell stories about their homeland. You might even try a cup of Greek coffee and baklava. Too bad there's no room for dancing.

Address
223 Bear Street
Banff

Phone
403.762.0377

Hours
Daily
11 am – 8 pm

Reservations
Not accepted

Cards
Cash only
ATM

Drinks
No alcoholic beverages

Takeout
Yes

Outdoor Dining
No

Website
No

The Big Cheese | Poutinerie

POUTINE has come a long way from its Quebec chip-wagon beginnings in the 1950s. It used to be a simple concoction of french fries, fresh cheese curds and a slightly tinny chicken-beef gravy (or poutine sauce, as some aficionados say it is called). But lately, haute poutineries have sprouted all over Canada, serving poutine topped with duck confit, rabbit rillette or even foie gras, as well as the curds and gravy.

There are many places to find poutine around here, but in the spring of 2011, Travis Burke, the entrepreneur behind The Drum & Monkey pub, opened Calgary's first dedicated poutinerie. He chose an appropriate spot, a century-old building that housed the first Nellie's cafe (which was named after suffragette Nellie McClung, whose former residence is just a short block away).

Following a major renovation, The Big Cheese opened with nineteen poutines, including the Notorious P.I.G. poutine topped with pulled pork, bacon and Italian sausage (along with the gravy and curds, of course) and a Peppercorn Chicken one covered in grilled chicken breast, sautéed mushrooms, caramelized onions and a green-peppercorn sauce. There are even three vegetarian poutines and Pop Shoppe pop. All poutines come in two sizes, and the top price is $10.

To achieve poutine excellence, Burke uses locally grown Yukon Gold potatoes. The potato strips are blanched in hot water, chilled and then fried twice in two different temperatures of oil to ensure their crispiness. And the curds are brought in straight from Quebec.

And the gravy? Well, that's a secret.

Address
738 – 17 Avenue SW

Phone
403.457.2873

Hours
Sunday – Thursday
11 am – closing

Friday & Saturday
11 am – 3:30 am

Reservations
Not accepted

Cards
V, MC, Debit

Drinks
No alcoholic beverages

Takeout
Yes

Outdoor Dining
Patio

Website
mybigcheese.com

Bistro Alma

Modern Casual

WHEN I attended the University of Calgary many years ago, my dining delights came largely from vending machines and a little basement cafeteria in Calgary (now Craigie) Hall. But with the opening of Hotel Alma in 2009, U of C dining was kicked up a notch.

The hotel is in International House, a new building that is part residence, part conference centre and part hotel, as in ninety-six rooms and suites rentable to anyone. On the ground floor, they included the forty-seat Bistro Alma, a sunny room appointed with sleek Phillipe Starck bar stools and orange Verner Panton chairs. It's modern and comfy at the same time.

Being a hotel cafe, Bistro Alma does three squares a day, including a continental breakfast and a lunch of soups, sandwiches, salads and comfort foods of beef bourguignon and pork tourtière. I've enjoyed a lunch of roasted red-peppers, pears and Brie on focaccia, preceded by a bowl of good onion soup, all for a reasonable $11. The dinner menu models the lunch one and both span the world with items like sushi rolls, Mac and Cheese, and bruschetta.

Nothing on any of the menus tops $14, and preparation is solid. One shortcoming is that much of the cooking is done at the university's main Dining Centre, so it can be a bit institutional—but they're trying hard to keep the quality up.

Which means it's waaay better than it was back in my day.

Address
169 University Gate NW
(University of Calgary)

Phone
403.220.3203

Hours
Monday – Friday
6:30 am – 11 pm

Saturday & Sunday
7 am – 11 pm

Holidays
8 am – 8 pm

Reservations
Accepted

Cards
V, MC, AE, Debit

Drinks
Fully licensed
No corkage

Takeout
Yes

Outdoor Dining
No

Website
hotelalma.ca

Blackfoot Diner

Diner

THE Blackfoot Diner has been around so long—since 1956—that my Dad remembers it from his trucking days. He'd haul truckloads of cattle to the Burns processing plant and then stop in for a meal before heading home to Wetaskiwin. Nowadays, Dad's long retired and the Burns plant has become the Crossroads Market, but the Blackfoot Diner is not only still open, it's still run by the same people.

Maybe that's why it seems locked in time, a place where Johnny Cash lives on in the jukebox and where knights of the road still park their eighteen-wheelers while they get some much-needed rest and grub. And where most of the staff have been there as long as the building. Likely the biggest change here is that the diner went non-smoking a few years ago when the law changed.

The food hasn't changed much, at least in my memory. This is the domain of hot turkey sandwiches smothered in gravy, griddle-cooked burgers, mile-high meringue pies and bottomless cups of coffee. Don't expect massive flavour from anything. Pepper is about as exotic a spice as you'll find. But do expect your meat to be cooked, your spuds mashed, your pie thick and filling. Want an espresso? Go somewhere else.

But it's a comfort that the Blackfoot always does it the Blackfoot way—that you can rely on the sameness of it. That's warming to me, just like a good rerun of an old *Wagon Train* episode.

Address
1840 – 9 Avenue SE

Phone
403.265.5964

Hours
Daily
24 hours a day

Reservations
Accepted

Cards
V, MC, AE, Debit
ATM at service centre

Drinks
Beer & wine only
No corkage

Takeout
Yes

Outdoor Dining
No

Website
No

Bon Appetit

THE South Airways Industrial Park is not exactly located in fine-dining central. The eateries here mostly hew to the chain variety or the anything-in-a-microwave style. But Bon Appetit is different.

It starts with the all-day breakfast using only free-range eggs. It ramps up with a selection of super-fresh salads doused with house-made dressings (including a fine, herb-filled balsamic vinaigrette), and it tops out with thick Monte Cristo or beef dip sandwiches. Then it finishes off with banana cream pie or a warm apple one topped with ice cream. And did I mention that almost nothing is over $10? (Both the hunter schnitzel and the beef strip loin are $12, but that's about it.)

What's most impressive about Bon Appetit is the food quality. It's very high for a restaurant in any part of town, and surprising for one in this fast-food area. I think that's because Bon Appetit's main business is catering to the businesses around them. So they use a lot of product every day, which helps keep things fresh. And to maintain the catering business, it has to be good.

On my last visit, I ordered a Denver sandwich, mostly because it's something we seldom see anymore. Lots of eggs, chopped ham, peppers, onions and Cheddar cheese on toasted brown bread. It was great—a simple, tasty reminiscence of the 1960s. And for $10, a bargain.

I'm also impressed with Bon Appetit's service—friendly, professional, swift and charming. That's always welcome in any area of town.

Address
8, 2915 – 19 Street NE

Phone
403.313.1152

Hours
Monday – Friday
7 am – 3 pm

Reservations
Accepted

Cards
V, MC, AE, Debit

Drinks
Fully licensed
No corkage

Takeout
Yes

Outdoor Dining
No

Website
bon-appetit.ca

Boogie's Burgers

Burgers

BOOGIE's Burgers has been around since the late 1960s, and in all that time, has had only four sets of owners. Each added something to the mix, but all have respected the past. So today, Boogie's has one foot in the 1960s with the other one stretched all the way into the 2010s.

Boogie's remains a throwback to the era when burgers were constructed individually to order. They still grill up the classic Sam's Burger (one patty, Cheddar, a fried egg, red sauce) from the second owner and the Keith's Burger (two patties, mushroom sauce, fried mushrooms and onions, pizza sauce, mozzarella, Cheddar, four bacon slices) from the third owner's son. (If you hadn't guessed, Keith was a teen when he invented his burger.) There are new varieties from the fourth owners, including Doug's "Don't Fear the Reaper" Burger of four patties, four bacon slices, two Cheddar slices, a fried egg, red sauce, a wiener…and a mini corn dog. (How do you eat that? And why?)

For those of smaller appetites, there's a good old, nameless single patty burger, plus all the fry varieties, onion rings and yam chips you would expect. Then there are the milkshakes—traditional ones like chocolate, vanilla or strawberry and "out there" flavours like bacon and maple syrup or cinnamon, cayenne and chocolate. I still think a good vanilla is hard to beat, but the PB and banana—also known as the Young Elvis—is pretty tempting. In any decade.

Address
908 Edmonton Trail NE

Phone
403.230.7070

Hours
Monday – Saturday
11 am – 9 pm

Sunday
Noon – 7 pm

Reservations
Accepted

Cards
V, MC, Debit

Drinks
Beer & wine only
Free corkage

Takeout
Yes

Outdoor Dining
4 picnic tables

Website
boogiesburgers.com

Boxwood

Local Sustainable

CAN it be that Boxwood, the little sister of River Café, known as one of Calgary's pricier (and more exquisite) restaurants, qualifies as a Cheap Eat? Especially when they serve spit-roasted porchetta sandwiches on house-made ciabatta, big bowls of BC halibut chowder with dill, carrots and potatoes, and a roasted organic chicken salad tossed with arugula and spinach and an arugula pesto?

Remarkably, that sandwich is $10, the chowder is $8 and the salad is $14, so Boxwood slips in under the wire for this book. At least if you go for lunch.

Head over for dinner and a slab of rotisserie-roasted lamb sided with a mint and anchovy salsa verde will cost $17. Add a side of roasted carrots with honey and thyme ricotta and that will be $7 more. (Oops. There goes the Cheap Eats budget. Still, though, pretty good prices for the quality.)

Boxwood adheres to River Café's regional, seasonal, sustainable focus. So they bring in good ingredients and treat them very well. That includes roasting almost everything, including vegetables, on their rotisserie.

Boxwood sits in Central Memorial Park, which was beautifully revived by The City recently. During the renos, two new buildings were constructed, one of which became Boxwood. It's a small but airy space that seats forty-two inside. With a few low tables, counters at the bar and along the windows, a high, communal table, and seating for more outside, it's meant for quick, casual meals.

All with a Cheap Eats price tag…at lunch.

Address
340 – 13 Avenue SW
(Central Memorial Park)

Phone
403.265.4006

Hours
Tuesday – Sunday
11 am – 10 pm

Reservations
Not accepted

Cards
V, MC, AE, Debit

Drinks
Fully licensed
Corkage $15 per bottle

Takeout
Yes

Outdoor Dining
Patio

Website
boxwoodcafe.ca

The British Chippy

IF a pair of yoga teachers and fitness instructors opened a restaurant, you might think there'd be sprouts and beans involved. But not so at the place Gary and Simone Hodgkinson opened. In 2009, the couple from Manchester opened…yep, a fish and chip shop. The closest you'll get to beans here is a serving of mushy peas.

Seems they were longing for a taste of the homeland, so since Gary is a fourth-generation fish fryer, they opened a small "chippy" (British lexicon for a fish and chip shop) and have been frying up cod and haddock ever since. But they do use organic potatoes to make their chips and their "smacks" (mmmm…battered and fried chips). And adding to the British theme, you can have a steak and kidney pie (from Calgary butcher shop MacEwan's Meats), a pot of tea, Lilt or Vimto (pops from the UK), a side order of curry sauce and, of course, the mushy peas.

The fish and chips are crisp and fairly light, perfect for splashing with a little lemon and/or malt vinegar. They're good fish and chips. (And unlike many British chippies, ketchup is available.)

Everything is made to order, so The British Chippy doesn't quite fit the mould of "fast food." Many fans have taken to calling ahead so their orders are ready when they arrive. But many others wait and enjoy the casual, almost pubbish tone of the place, especially if there's an episode of *Coronation Street* on the telly.

Address
233, 2335 – 162 Avenue SW
(Shoppes at Bridlewood)

Phone
403.256.1156

Hours
Wednesday – Saturday
11:30 am – 2 pm

Wednesday – Sunday
4:30 pm – 8 pm

Reservations
Not accepted

Cards
V, MC, AE, Debit

Drinks
Beer & wine only
No corkage

Takeout
Yes

Outdoor Dining
No

Website
thebritishchippy.com

Bumpy's

Look down the alley on 8th Street SW, between 10th and 11th Avenues (between Bonterra and Brewsters, if that helps) and take a sniff. Smell coffee? Good coffee? Now follow your nose up some steps and open the door to Bumpy's. Careful—you're heading for a full-on coffee-house assault.

Bumpy's will be filled with people, some lined up to order, others waiting for their coffees to-go, more seated at tables. It'll be noisy, what with the espresso grinders and hubbub of conversation. It'll smell good, the coffee more intense inside and the scent of fresh muffins or soup sneaking into your nostrils between whiffs of cappuccino.

Watch where you stand—there'll be more Bumpites coming in behind you needing their fix. And they'll be headed right for the ordering station. Stay out of their line of traffic. Look up at the overhead blackboard menus instead. Peer into the display cases filled with pastries and sandwiches. Now make a decision. Quiche? Chili? Panini? Muffin? Carrot cake?

Step up to the cashier and place your order. Coffee. Food. Take your table marker and move along. Try to find a free table or chair. Settle in for a moment and your order will arrive, delivered by a smiling server.

Time to indulge. Sip. Savour. Take a bite. Enjoy. Repeat.

Enjoy the room, too—the pastel 1950s-meets-modern-coffee-house setting—plus the energy, the staff and the eclectic melange of regulars. Next time, you'll know what to do. You'll be a Bumpite, too.

Address
1040 – 8 Street SW

Phone
403.265.0244

Hours
Monday – Friday
6:30 am – 5 pm

Saturday & Sunday
7:30 am – 4 pm

Reservations
Not accepted

Cards
V, MC, Debit

Drinks
No alcoholic beverages

Takeout
Yes

Outdoor Dining
Deck

Website
bumpyscafe.com

Byblos Deli

Middle Eastern

I F you've lived in Calgary for more than, say, ten minutes, there's a pretty good chance you've bitten into a Byblos pita. For over thirty-five years, it's been the go-to pita for Middle Eastern restaurants, business-lunch caterers, party planners and anyone who's looked for bread to spread with hummus or stuff with falafel. And since they moved into their northeast bakery in 1988, they've rolled out reams of bagels and tortillas, too.

Byblos has had a retail outlet at their bakery since that Olympic year, but in 2009, they expanded it into a full-blown deli. So if you're buzzing past on Barlow Trail and are in need of some zataar manakeesh (pitas covered in olive oil and a mix of dried herbs) or fatayers (triangular-shaped, savoury stuffed pastries) or a falafel sandwich, you can pop in any day of the week. The falafel is great—cooked through to a crunchy goodness. And the hummus is rich and creamy and less garlicky than some.

You can even take a dine-in break here at one of the tables situated between the tall racks of bread. The trouble with dining in is that you'll be staring at all the lovely Middle Eastern sweets, including baklava done three ways—with either pistachios, cashews or hazelnuts. And once you see them, you'll want them. The big question is, can you stop at one? (Maybe just one of each—that's fair.)

Address
2479 – 23 Street NE

Phone
403.219.1359

Hours
Daily
9 am – 5 pm

Reservations
Not accepted

Cards
V, MC, AE, Debit

Drinks
No alcoholic beverages

Takeout
Yes

Outdoor Dining
Patio

Website
byblosbakery.com

Cadence

21st Century Diner

I COULD say that Cadence is located in the heart of Bowness, but I don't think that says it quite right. Perhaps it's better to say that Cadence *is* the heart of Bowness.

For over ten years, Cadence has been pulling primo Oso Negro espresso (from Nelson, BC) and serving huge Rice Krispies squares and muffins and those other sweet squares packed with miniature—and multi-coloured—marshmallows. They've produced a long list of breakfast dishes that range from straight-up bacon and eggs to parfaits of yogurt and fruit, with variations like perogies and kolbassa (now that's a breakfast!) in between. They've got lunch sandwiches and salads, and recently, they've extended their hours into the late afternoon to satisfy those who want to grab something on the way home from work.

But Cadence has also become a community centre, a place where biking and walking groups, area seniors, students and commuters gather. Folks linger over coffee or lunch, grab a newspaper and catch up on community activities. Everyone's welcome. We even took a wedding party here one afternoon when we had a few hours between the service and the reception.

Cadence does all this in a space that is appropriately, well, Bownessian. It's painted in funky colours, and the outlandish paintings covering the walls are, shall we say, interesting. The tables may rock a bit on the checkerboard floor, and there's still angle parking outside.

Seems like the heart of the community to me.

Address
6407 Bowness Road NW

Phone
403.247.9955

Hours
Monday – Friday
7 am – 6 pm

Saturday & Sunday
8 am – 5 pm

Reservations
Not accepted

Cards
V, MC, Debit

Drinks
No alcoholic beverages

Takeout
Yes

Outdoor Dining
3 benches

Website
cadencecoffee.com

Caffè Beano

CAFFÈ Beano has been here long enough to be considered an institution. Over the past two decades, it's evolved from a tiny, upstart coffee joint to a slightly larger place for coffee aficionados to an even larger coffee house that anchors a stretch of 17th Avenue SW. And I swear some of the folks hanging out on the benches in front have been there since Day One. Sometimes the staff are a bit distracted, but let's just say they bring a charming individuality to the business.

Beano has gained great loyalty for its locally roasted Fratello coffee. They do all the current espresso drinks and foam art, and they do it with what they call an "old school" approach, referring to the fact that they use a blend of beans for their rich, dark caffeine hit rather than a single estate bean.

Beyond Beano's caffeinated products, there's a respectable list of foods, sourced from local producers like Wayne's Bagels, Gull Valley Greenhouses and Hoven Farms. A sandwich using Manuel Latruwe's baguette and next-door neighbour Janice Beaton's fine ham and cheese is as good as most similar sandwiches I've had in France. And the in-house baked muffins are some of the best in the city. (The really dark one made with molasses is my favourite—great with an espresso.)

So Beano continues to evolve, but at the same time, stays the same. Through several owners, it's always maintained the quality. That's as comforting as their hot chocolate.

Address
1613 – 9 Street SW

Phone
403.229.1232

Hours
Monday – Friday
6 am – midnight

Saturday & Sunday
7 am – midnight

Reservations
Not accepted

Cards
Debit

Drinks
No alcoholic beverages

Takeout
Yes

Outdoor Dining
6 benches

Website
caffebeano.ca

Caffè Mauro

Italian Cafe

FANS have followed Sal Malvaso around for years. He's cooked at big places and little places and even had his own downtown cafe (or should I say caffè) on 1st Street for a while. Never one to let the espresso grow cold under his feet, though, he moved his Caffè Mauro a couple of years ago to a spot across from Mountain Equipment Co-op.

Malvaso likes the regular hours he has here. No evenings, no weekends—the bane of existence for many a chef. And he likes his simple menu of mostly Italian sandwiches, all custom made and carefully prepared by him.

Caffè Mauro is a plain, thirty-six-seat space on the main floor of an office tower, and at first glance, there doesn't appear to be enough food to make a sandwich. But order a meatball panini and Malvaso will slice open his handmade focaccia, layer in steaming meatballs, roasted peppers, mushrooms and provolone, and press it all in a panini grill. With a bowl of soup (maybe his thick, creamy mushroom), you'll have a lunch to satisfy your every taste bud. Ask for a simple prosciutto sandwich and you'll be faced with added options like roasted eggplant, grilled mushrooms, olive tapenade and bocconcini, with maybe a fresh-tossed salad on the side.

In keeping with the name, Malvaso pulls Italian espresso, made from Mauro coffee, of course. So get one of those before heading back to work—you'll knock it back before it grows cold, too.

Address
999 – 8 Street SW

Phone
403.277.7572

Hours
Monday – Friday
7 am – 4 pm

Reservations
Accepted

Cards
Debit

Drinks
No alcoholic beverages

Takeout
Yes

Outdoor Dining
Patio

Website
No

Chicken on the Way

Fried Chicken

You may have chuckled to yourself when you saw this entry and thought, "Chicken on the Way? Seriously?" Yes, seriously.

COTW has been around since 1958, so they must be doing something right. They fry up over 2,000 chickens each and every week, and they scoop about 10,000 corn fritters and chop 5,000 pounds of potatoes in the same amount of time. (I checked the numbers.) And they pack the chicken, the fries and the fritters into their signature yellow-and-red cardboard boxes for immediate car dining, and for a take-home delight, they wrap up the boxes in brown paper. (Make sure you ask them to toss in the vinegar and ketchup before wrapping—they don't do it automatically.)

COTW is a family-run operation—the same family since Day One. They used to own the farm that produces the chickens, too. They don't anymore, but they still get their birds there.

And as quick take-away fried chicken goes, it's pretty good. It's not as greasy or salty as some of the big brands and it's crispy and fairly meaty, just the way they did it in 1958. The Bonus Order—three pieces of chicken, fries, one fritter and a choice of gravy or slaw for $7.25—is the top choice. You can add another fritter for 45 cents. And seriously—who doesn't want an extra fritter?

When I whiz by on 14th Street, there's almost always a lineup, and I always want to stop. Seriously. You know you do, too.

Address
1443 Kensington Road NW

Phone
403.283.5545

Hours
Monday – Thursday
10:30 am – 12:30 am

Friday & Saturday
10:30 am – 1:30 am

Sunday
10:30 am – 11 pm

Reservations
Not accepted
(No indoor seating)

Cards
V, MC, Debit

Drinks
No alcoholic beverages

Takeout
Yes
Delivery

Outdoor Dining
2 picnic tables

Website
No

Chuckwagon

Western Diner

Some day I'm going to have Chuckwagon's vaunted flatiron-steak eggs Benedict. Twice now I've driven out to Turner Valley and ordered the Benny with the slice of steak and been told they were out of it that day.

Now I understand that they don't use just any flatiron steak. Owner Terry Myhre raises his own cattle, then dry-ages the beef twenty-four days before serving it in his restaurant. So when they're out, they're out. C'est la vie.

And sure, I could have a burger made from that same beef or a steak sandwich or whatever cut is being served in the steak and eggs that day, but when your palate is set on flatiron-steak eggs Benedict, those just don't work. So I've had the regular Benedict with hollandaise on a toasted croissant both times. And it's great. Perfect eggs, creamy smooth hollandaise, nice touch with the croissant.

But given the setting, I want that flatiron. I look at Clint Eastwood glaring at me from the *Unforgiven* poster (which was shot in the area, of course) and know that he would want me to have the beef Benny. I look away and hear Ian Tyson warbling on the stereo. What would that local-hero-cum-rancher think of my croissant? And over in the corner, there's one of those stand-up posters of the Alberta cowgirls with the classic quote, "If it ain't Alberta, it ain't beef."

Well, maybe third time lucky.

Address
105 Sunset Boulevard SW
Turner Valley

Phone
403.933.0003

Hours
Monday – Friday
8 am – 2:30 pm

Saturday & Sunday
8 am – 3:30 pm

Reservations
Not accepted

Cards
V, MC, Debit

Drinks
No alcoholic beverages

Takeout
Yes

Outdoor Dining
Patio

Website
chuckwagoncafe.ca

Clay Oven

Indian (Punjabi)

THERE have been changes at Clay Oven. Original owner Gurnek Gill has retired and passed his restaurant on to son Balpreet and long-time staffer Bindu Dhaliwal. But even though that's a pretty big change, Clay Oven remains practically the same.

That's because Balpreet spent much of his youth in the restaurant (it opened in 1997 when he was sixteen), and he learned the food secrets directly from his father. So the cuisine, from the lunchtime buffet to the long list of dinner dals and curries, has stayed remarkably the same. And in the dining room, Dhaliwal has been filling and emptying the buffet and the gaggle of tables for over a decade, so service has not missed a beat either. Sure, the buffet has gone up a buck to $13 (a bargain), but that's life.

A further point of stability is having the same bread baker since 1999. That's a deal breaker for many customers. Good as the buffet is and as divine as the lamb karahi and aloo gobi of cauliflower and potatoes are, it's the breads that take Clay Oven over the top. From the thin, unleavened chapati and the spiced-onion kulcha to the buttery paratha and the simple, fluffy baked nan, Clay Oven serves the best Indian bread in town. Regardless of how many Indian restaurants there are, I have yet to find better breads.

I should mention another constant at Clay Oven—the traffic jam at the buffet. But I guess that's life, too.

Address
349, 3132 – 26 Street NE

Phone
403.250.2161

Hours
Monday – Friday
11:30 am – 2 pm

Monday – Thursday
5 pm – 8:30 pm

Friday & Saturday
5 pm – 9:30 pm

Reservations
Recommended

Cards
V, MC, Debit

Drinks
Fully licensed
Corkage $10 per bottle

Takeout
Yes
Delivery

Outdoor Dining
No

Website
clayovencalgary.com

Communitea

New Age Cafe

WHENEVER I want to find out what's happening in Canmore, I drop into Communitea for lunch, a cup of tea or a shot of espresso. In its few short years, Communitea has become a focus for local activity—a destination for business or social meetings or a place to catch up on local happenings. So Communitea is a good name for this sixty-five-seat cafe.

Communitea does breakfast and lunch daily, but that's far from all they do. Many nights a week, they also open the doors for ticketed concerts. It's a busy place.

But it's also one of the most relaxing places in town. They have a great tea selection here, including ten black ones—my favourite—plus good Intelligentsia espresso. So if I sink into a beanbag chair with a cup of Himalayan Estate Darjeeling and a chicken breast, goat cheese and fig jam panini, I may not rise for hours. Unless I need a refill. Or if I tuck into a bowl of pad Thai noodles and gaze out at the mountains, I know I'll feel as de-stressed as if I were visiting a spa. With a lower price tag.

Everything at Communitea is under $15. Sure, it's simple stuff, but there's creativity. The green eggs and ham panini, for example, is made with Valbella ham, Gruyère, spinach and basil pesto. And there are many vegetarian and vegan options.

Plus the feeling of community at Communitea. That's priceless.

Address
117, 1001 – 6 Avenue
Canmore

Phone
403.678.6818

Hours
Monday – Friday
9 am – 4 pm

Saturday & Sunday
9 am – 5 pm

Reservations
Not accepted

Cards
V, MC, Debit

Drinks
Fully licensed
Corkage $15 per bottle

Takeout
Yes

Outdoor Dining
Small patio

Website
thecommunitea.com

Cowtown Beef Shack

BLINK when you're passing Home Food Inn's parking lot and you'll miss Cowtown Beef Shack—it takes longer to say the name than it does to drive by this tiny (as in, less than ten-square-metres tiny) hut. The shack started life years ago as a drive-through coffee bar, but in more recent days, has become a vendor of many tasty Angus AAA roast beef sandwiches. And in even more recent days, it has also started offering sandwiches of brisket and pulled pork (soon there will be a cranberry-apple coleslaw, too).

Bradley Johnson had the idea to open Cowtown after enjoying the roast beef sandwiches sold on the Stampede Grounds during the yearly rodeo. He figured folks would like that sandwich the other 355 days of the year, too. So he worked up some saucy recipes to add to his roast beef sandwiches, bought the hut, buffed it up and opened it as Cowtown.

The place looks good inside with all its shiny stainless steel pots and slicers and its new barbecue smoker. There's even an airplane-sized bathroom in the back. Dine-in options consist of eating in your vehicle or…eating in your vehicle. It's either that or hunker down at one of seven picnic tables on a grassy (or snowy) boulevard along Macleod Trail.

It's tasty, hefty stuff, even if you choose the smallest sandwich. And smoky if you go for the pork or brisket. And messy, especially if you opt for both barbecue and cheese sauce instead of the simple au jus beef version. Overkill? Maybe, but you know you want one.

Address
5250 Macleod Trail S

Phone
403.281.8191

Hours
Daily
11 am – 8 pm

Reservations
Not accepted
(No indoor seating)

Cards
V, MC, Debit

Drinks
No alcoholic beverages

Takeout
Yes
Delivery

Outdoor Dining
7 picnic tables

Website
cowtownbeefshack.com

Cultural Centre

FROM the outside it looks quiet enough. But descend the stairs of the Calgary Chinese Cultural Centre and you'll be greeted by a wall of noise, especially at lunchtime. Inside a cavernous room, up to 350 people will be chowing down on a buffet ($11) or diving into dim sum steamers. (At night, there's a hot pot buffet—pick your foods and cook them in your own hot pot for $19, or order off a very long, mostly Cantonese menu, which is available throughout the day, too.)

The dim sum lunch is a delight. You order off a dim sum menu where servings run mostly $4 to $6. (No dim sum carts here.) There are oodles of steamed dumplings and rice rolls and short ribs and such. The order in which they'll be delivered is arbitrary; it depends on what the cooks have going on in the kitchen.

The flavours are generally mild and light at the Cultural Centre Restaurant, in keeping with Cantonese cuisine, but if you want to kick it up a notch, you can try the weekday lunch buffet. There you'll find Shanghai, Singaporean and even Korean dishes. And, of course, ginger beef. (I don't think it's legal to have a Chinese buffet in Calgary without ginger beef.)

The Cultural Centre Restaurant prides itself on preparing everything in-house, and certainly with the number of people coming through each day, everything seems very fresh. And very loud.

Address
88, 197 – 1 Street SW
(Lower Level, Calgary
Chinese Cultural Centre)

Phone
403.457.0072

Hours
Monday – Friday
10 am – 11 pm

Saturday
9 am – 11 pm

Sunday & Holidays
9 am – 10 pm

Reservations
Recommended

Cards
V, MC, Debit

Drinks
Fully licensed
Corkage $10 per bottle

Takeout
Yes
Delivery

Outdoor Dining
No

Website
culturalcentrerestaurant.com

Dairy Lane | Diner

Wɪᴛʜ a legacy dating back to 1950, Dairy Lane is perhaps the second-oldest restaurant in the city. (Almost no eateries in these parts predate the Second World War. FYI, the Palliser Hotel's Rimrock is the oldest, opening as it did in 1914.) Anyway, Dairy Lane has had a few changes over the years, but remains true to its size and its West Hillhurst neighbourhood. It was my go-to joint for ragged mornings-after during my U of C days. A quick breakfast, endless coffee and non-judgemental service would help set me on the straight and narrow.

These days, Dairy Lane is all spruced up and retro, with a patio where the takeout window used to be. It's now under the stewardship of Shayne and Jodi Perrin, who are strongly committed to local producers—check out the long list of names on the menu and website.

The food straddles the line between classic diner fare and contemporary but rustic choices. They have three kinds of veggie burgers, for Pete's sake, in addition to a pork burger, a turkey burger, and yes, a beef burger. There's a good beer and cocktail list and even international flavours of jerk-spiced tofu, curried chicken salad and chorizo-laden omelettes.

But most of all, there's still a great breakfast at Dairy Lane, with options ranging from hot oats and flax with organic sugar and berry compote to stuffed French toast to eggs, any style, with bacon, sausage, hash browns and toast. Some things just can't be improved on.

Address
319 – 19 Street NW

Phone
403.283.2497

Hours
Monday & Tuesday
7 am – 3 pm

Wednesday – Friday
7 am – 8 pm

Saturday & Sunday
8 am – 8 pm

Reservations
Accepted after 4 pm

Cards
V, MC, Debit

Drinks
Fully licensed
No corkage

Takeout
When possible

Outdoor Dining
Patio

Website
dairylanecafe.ca

Diner Deluxe

Contemporary Diner

I'M having a hard time writing about Diner Deluxe right now. I'm at my computer, unshaven, wearing my ratty "I ♥ NY" T-shirt, tapping away with only a few scrappy pieces of toast in my stomach. I know I'm going to have to glance over at their menu in a few minutes and memories of their good food are going to come flooding back.

I'll read about those buckwheat-muesli pancakes with maple butter or the veal meat loaf with Dijon-mashed potatoes, grilled vegetables, pan gravy and red-pepper jelly. Or about the four kinds of eggs Benedict or the sourdough French toast stuffed with bacon and Gouda.

And I'll start thinking about the great fifties decor. My mind will wander to the counter where you can see the cooks melting white Cheddar onto big beefy burgers or sliding scrambled eggs onto a tortilla with jalapeno jack cheese and salsa. I'll remember the whir of the milkshake machine churning shakes from house-made ice cream and the smell of pulled pork sandwiches being doused with chipotle barbecue sauce.

So…a few minutes have passed. I've read the menu and I'm really hungry. If it were a weekday, I would be changing into a clean T-shirt, jumping in my car and heading up Edmonton Trail to DD. But it's the weekend, so I'm just letting out a sad sigh and thinking about the lineup that is likely snaking out the door. And I'll get back to work until the line shortens.

Address
804 Edmonton Trail NE

Phone
403.276.5499

Hours
Monday – Friday
7:30 am – 9:30 pm

Saturday
8 am – 3 pm
5 pm – 9:30 pm

Sunday
8 am – 3 pm

Reservations
Accepted for groups of 6 or more after 5 pm

Cards
V, MC, AE, Debit

Drinks
Fully licensed
Corkage $20 per bottle
Free corkage Wednesdays

Takeout
Weekdays only

Outdoor Dining
Patio

Website
dinerdeluxe.com

eat! eat! in Inglewood

INGLEWOOD is fast becoming Calgary's most eclectic dining neighbourhood. From blues bars and organic bakeries to premium restaurants and down-and-dirty diners, it seems to have it all. And at all price ranges, too. But one place has a real corner on the breakfast market—eat! eat! in Inglewood. (Maybe it's the exclamation marks that attract people!!)

Seriously, I think it's the almost-all-day (until 3 pm) approach to breakfast that draws folks. I mean, what's wrong with breakfast after lunch? Works for me. The breakfast menu is mostly made up of omelettes and French toast, Benedicts and porridge (steel-cut oats rule!), with a steak-and-eggs option for $15—that's an eight-ounce New York with home fries, toast and two eggs. And coffee is organic fair trade. (You didn't even have to ask that did you?)

eat! eat! is a comfortable place with sixty-six seats spread over two rooms and CKUA almost always on the airwaves. It's an old building—it's in Inglewood after all—with wooden floors and tables that don't quite balance.

And if your preference runs to lunch instead of breakfast, they've got burgers (including a veggie one loaded with hemp hearts), lasagna, salads, beef dips and a build-your-own-sandwich option. Desserts are listed daily and include house-made pies. And alcoholic beverages are served after 10 am. (No wine with my pancakes? Well, maybe that's a good idea. It is eat! eat! after all—not drink! drink!)

Homestyle Meals

Address
1325 – 9 Avenue SE

Phone
403.532.1933

Hours
Monday – Friday
7 am – 3 pm

Saturday & Sunday
8 am – 4 pm

Holidays
9 am – 3 pm

Reservations
Accepted weekdays only

Cards
V, MC, Debit

Drinks
Fully licensed
No corkage

Takeout
Yes

Outdoor Dining
No

Website
No

Falafel King

Mediterranean

WHEN it comes to cheap and quick food options downtown, they are few and far between, at least for anything you'd actually want to eat. So it's great to see that Falafel King still reigns supreme over a small principality on Stephen Avenue. And that the King has so many loyal subjects.

The current Falafel King is remarkably discreet. The original location had a huge gold crown as a marquee. This cafe is only a few metres wide, yet still they come, hungry customers drawn in by just the right heady aroma of spit-roasted meats. And by the spinach or potato fatayer, the kibbeh of ground beef, spices and cracked wheat, the salads and, of course, the falafel.

Wedge your way inside during a workday lunch hour and you'll see a long line of people waiting patiently for their orders. Some of them will find seats inside, but many more will take their food back to the office, tempting their co-workers with the scent of tahini or garlic sauce. It's fragrant stuff. Many will also carry one of Falafel King's fresh juices—orange, apple, carrot or maybe strawberry or mango—whatever is fresh and seasonal and in whatever combination they'd like. The juices may not be potent enough to wash away the lingering garlic of a sandwich, but they do make a great complement to the food. And they are a fine way to attract new subjects.

Address
225 Stephen Avenue SW

Phone
403.269.5464

Hours
Monday – Saturday
10 am – 8 pm

Reservations
Accepted

Cards
V, MC, AE, Debit

Drinks
No alcoholic beverages

Takeout
Yes

Outdoor Dining
No

Website
falafelking.ca

Famoso

Neapolitan Pizza

I DON'T typically include chain restaurants in my books, but Famoso isn't quite a chain—yet. There are a number of outlets in Edmonton and only this one in Calgary. So far.

Famoso is lively and loud and has a bit of a cafeteria tone. Ordering can be a bit confusing—you first find a seat, you next go to the counter to order and you then head back to your seat to be served. Drinks will be replenished and desserts ordered at your table. Don't worry—it usually works out. Entertainment consists of watching your pizza stretched and loaded into the oven or spying on other patrons to figure out the ordering system.

Famoso does the soft-crust, cooked-in-ninety-seconds, Neapolitan-style pizza. They use finely milled Italian flour, tomatoes from the Campania region of Italy, fior di latte mozzarella and fresh basil, and they hand-stretch each pie to about eleven inches. There are the traditional ones like margherita or quattro formaggi, plus their New World ones with toppings like barbecued chicken or Italian ham and crushed pineapple (yep, pineapple). It's good pizza all round if you like a foldable crust.

There are also salads, sandwiches on fresh-baked bread, soups and a remarkably reasonable wine list. No pizza is over $14.50, and there are very drinkable wines under $30. (That's right, under $30.)

It's controlled chaos, but then, you're not here for a long evening. Famoso is about good food, fast and cheap. Which is what this book is all about, too.

Address
105, 2303 – 4 Street SW

Phone
403.455.3839

Hours
Daily
11 am – 11 pm

Reservations
Accepted for groups of 8 or more except Friday & Saturday after 4 pm

Cards
V, MC, AE, Debit

Drinks
Fully licensed
Corkage $15 per bottle

Takeout
Yes

Outdoor Dining
No

Website
famoso.ca

Fat City Franks

Gourmet Hot Dogs

CAN it be that my favourite milkshake is at a hot dog joint? Fat City Franks, the little gourmet dog shop in Mission that used to be called Le Chien Chaud, makes their milkshakes old-school, with malted milk powder. That may well be a taste I acquired at the Tastee-Freez of my youth, and it's one I seem to be sticking to. A good malted vanilla milkshake (yes siree, I'm a vanilla kinda guy) is a joy to behold and taste—it's thick, creamy and malty. And that's just how Fat City does them.

But hey, Fat City Franks is mainly about hot dogs. Specifically, five different kinds of wieners, from bison to vegetarian ones. Choose yours and then decide from a list of over a dozen different themes, from the Mexican dog topped with jalapeno mustard, salsa fresca, banana peppers, Cheddar and cilantro to the French dog topped with butter-sautéed mushrooms, herbes de Provence, Gruyère and Dijon. I'm partial to the Chicago dog with its kosher dill, tomatoes, cucumbers, celery salt and sport pepper. A good dog, fine toppings and a great crusty bun. (You can also top your dog your own way.)

Fat City is a cute joint, too, reminiscent of a fifties diner. There are eighteen seats tucked into the compact room, a family-friendly space that provides a great view onto the passing foot traffic of 4th Street.

So, a dog of your choice, a malted milkshake and primo people watching, all for about $10. Does it get any better?

Address
3, 2015 – 4 Street SW

Phone
403.229.3641

Hours
Monday – Saturday
11 am – 8 pm

Sunday
Noon – 5 pm

Reservations
Not accepted

Cards
V, MC, Debit

Drinks
No alcoholic beverages

Takeout
Yes

Outdoor Dining
No

Website
fatcityfranks.com

Fat Kee

FAT Kee threw me for a loop on my last visit. I've always recommended first-timers grab a copy of the takeout menu on the way *in* so they know what to order before they're even seated. This place is so fast—and, to be honest, impatient—that you don't have a lot of time to dwell on choices. Regulars often order—by number—as they walk to their tables. Maybe the #79 (fried rice noodles with chicken in black-bean sauce) or the #51 (salt-and-pepper shrimp) or the #54 (sweet-and-sour spareribs).

But last time I went…gulp…there were no menus by the door. They'd run out. What to do? What to do? Should I play menu roulette and just reel off a couple of random numbers, hoping to get something I'd like? Or, like a rube newbie, should I ask for a real menu? Panic!

And then…inspiration. Spying a plate of steaming noodles and seafood on someone else's table, I said to the server, "That looks good. I'll have that." At first, I think she wondered if I wanted that specific plate, but she sorted it out and brought me my own plate of Shanghai fried noodles with shrimp, squid and scallops. Whew—it worked out. For only $9, I was happy.

Fat Kee is not the best Chinese food around. But it is definitely tasty. And it's hot, cheap and extremely fast. Menu or not.

Address
345, 3132 – 26 Street NE

Phone
403.250.8436

Hours
Monday – Saturday
11 am – 10 pm

Reservations
Accepted

Cards
V, MC

Drinks
Beer only
No corkage

Takeout
Yes
Delivery

Outdoor Dining
No

Website
No

F.A.T.S.

F.A.T.S. Gotta love the name. It stands for Fifth Avenue Tenth Street, the location of this Sunnyside bar and grill. Someone was very smart about that.

That same smartness flows over into the operation itself. It's a pleasant, bright room—for a bar. I mean, it's mostly black and brown, filled with tall tables on a polished concrete floor, surrounded by televisions spewing sports. Yeah, it's pretty much a guy place.

The menu follows suit with every bar dish possible, from dry ribs and wings (in a choice of ten sauces) to burgers, fish and chips, and pizzas. But look further and you'll find a list of salads including one of spinach, dried cranberries and almonds in a vanilla-cranberry vinaigrette topped with a Brie crostini. (Hmmm—does that go with a pint of Kokanee?) There's also a sweet-potato and bacon chowder, a barbecued chicken wrap and bruschetta. It's an eclectic mix.

And well executed. I tried a superb black-bean and green-pea soup with smoked ham. It was a creamy preamble to a beef dip that was very tender and topped with sautéed mushrooms and mozzarella. I was impressed. And for $12 all in, a fine lunch for a great price.

I was impressed with other details, too. The cutlery is high quality and the food is served on the same big, white plates that more expensive places use.

Seems F.A.T.S. has a lot of good thinking behind it.

Address
506 – 10 Street NW

Phone
403.270.3525

Hours
Daily
11 am – midnight

Reservations
Accepted

Cards
V, MC, Debit
ATM

Drinks
Fully licensed
No corkage

Takeout
Yes

Outdoor Dining
No

Website
fatsbarandgrill.com

Fire Kirin

When the smiling server described the daily special of Malaysian laksa, I ordered it immediately. A big bowl of curry-coconut broth loaded with noodles, shrimp, chicken and greens, it sounded like khao soi, a curry-coconut-noodle soup I've loved in Chiangmai, Thailand. You can find it in almost any restaurant there, but none of the Thai restaurants in Calgary do it. (One explained to me that they would need a chef from Chiangmai to do it right.)

Regardless, the laksa here tasted great. The creamy broth was just spicy enough, the chicken and shrimp tender, the noodles plentiful and the tofu thankfully innocuous. For $9, it was a meal in itself for one person.

I was equally impressed with the rest of our dishes, which gave nods to Vietnamese, Chinese and Japanese cuisines: grilled salmon salad rolls ($7); string beans with shiitake mushrooms and a spicy bean paste called tobanjan ($10); and jumbo prawns wok-fried in garlic, sake and salt and then served over caramelized onions ($15). Sure, our dinner was close to the $20 limit of this book, but we had leftovers for lunch.

Fire Kirin is a family-run operation—the father is in the kitchen, the mother and a daughter are out front—and when things get busy, more family members are called in to assist. One more note: The wine is all from Mission Hill. The family visited the Kelowna winery and liked it, so Mission Hill it is. That suits me fine.

Address
12101 Lake Fraser Drive SE
(Avenida Place)

Phone
403.278.8018

Hours
Monday – Saturday
11 am – 2 pm

Monday – Thursday &
Sunday
4:30 pm – 10 pm

Friday & Saturday
4:30 pm – 11 pm

Reservations
Recommended

Cards
V, MC, AE, Debit

Drinks
Fully licensed
Corkage $15 per bottle

Takeout
Yes
Delivery

Outdoor Dining
No

Website
firekirin.ca

The Flat Crepe & Cafe

Crepes

I LIKE restaurant names that relate to the food (like Tubby Dog) or the surroundings (like Flatlands). Right away, then, I like The Flat Crepe & Cafe. I mean, have you ever seen a crepe that wasn't flat? And since this spot is located in the topographically challenged neighbourhood of Woodbine, the whole "flat" idea works. So given the moniker, I'm already predisposed to liking this place.

And I like the food, too. Ilden Loyola and Paul Sartori have put together an attractive menu of crepes that runs from breakfast through to dinner, with a detour into dessert. Both the savoury and the sweet crepes are made with wheat flour—no buckwheat flour for the savoury ones like traditionally used in France.

Fillings range from ham and egg to smoked salmon, capers, asparagus and Boursin cheese, with a Peking duck, cucumber and hoisin-sauce version in between. On the sweet side, there's a combo of strawberries, banana and chocolate or a simple raspberry and crème fraîche, among others. If crepes aren't to your liking, most of the menu choices can be squeezed into the panini press between slices of locally made Prairie Mill bread. (Probably not the raspberries and crème fraîche, I'm thinking, or the strawberries and banana.)

As far as decor goes, there isn't much— it's a strip-mall bay with two small seating areas. But look for the owners to open more locations around town. Maybe even in the hilly parts. Wonder if they'll have to change the name then?

Address
201, 2525 Woodview Drive SW

Phone
403.984.3528

Hours
Monday – Friday
7 am – 8 pm

Saturday & Sunday
9 am – 5 pm

Reservations
Accepted

Cards
Debit

Drinks
No alcoholic beverages

Takeout
Yes

Outdoor Dining
No

Website
No

Flatlands

IN a world of breakfast and coffee chains, it's heartening to find a few that strike an independent pose and do it their own way. Places like Flatlands.

I love the name. The two non-native Calgarians who run Flatlands—Andrew Blevins and Brent Robinson—looked at the Foothills, the Rockies and the Prairies around Calgary and named their cafe after the feature that impressed them the most. Ergo, Flatlands.

But there's nothing flat about what's going on inside this place. House-baked scones and muffins and cookies that melt in your mouth (seriously, you've got to be quick or all those chocolate chips will melt in your hand). Thick sandwiches made of roasted, thinly sliced bison or beef, stacked high on rye bread with coleslaw on the side. Serious salads like the Cobb laden with avocado, flat-leaf parsley, roasted turkey, bacon, egg, tomato, leaf lettuce and crumbled blue cheese. (Doesn't that sound good?) Big cups of dark-roasted coffee. (No espresso machine here—just the drip stuff.)

This is sincere food, made by the people who are serving it to you. They like to feed people, and they do it with care. Customers notice. Many are moving quickly but seriously on their way to and from work. After a brief visit to Flatlands, though, they leave with lifts in their steps and smiles on their faces.

Good food can do that to you. Good people can, too.

Address
550 – 11 Avenue SW
(Pattison Square)

Phone
403.265.7144

Hours
Monday – Friday
7 am – 2 pm

Reservations
Accepted

Cards
V, MC, AE, Debit

Drinks
No alcoholic beverages

Takeout
Yes

Outdoor Dining
Small patio

Website
flatlandscafe.com

My Favourite Cheap Eats 2 | John Gilchrist   35

Fresh Delicious

Contemporary Deli

Slice Serrano ham and Manchego cheese and layer them into crusty bread with roasted red peppers and smoked paprika aioli and, my bet is, people will beat a rapid path to your door. Do the same with sliced turkey, smoked cheese, apples and a grainy mustard mayo and you'll build a big fan base. Add in a bowl of smoking-hot beef and vegetable soup, a dill pickle and some chips, keep the whole thing well under $15 and you'll have them coming back day after day.

That seems to be the plan at Fresh Delicious, a bright new development on Stephen Avenue. They've taken over a long, narrow storefront that used to house a currency exchange and have turned it into a delightful deli.

The dining process is simple. Pick your breakfast or lunch from an overhead chalkboard, order at the counter, find a seat and wait for your food. The toughest part is deciding what you want.

There are a number of great sandwiches such as the roast beef and Cheddar or the grilled vegetables with garlic-flower cream cheese or the two mentioned above. There are salads like quinoa with black beans, corn, tomatoes, almonds and olives or orzo with pine nuts, lemon zest, feta and green onions. You can tell that some serious thought has gone into these recipes.

And I for one am happy to see such thoughtfulness.

Address
112B Stephen Avenue SW

Phone
403.453.0304

Hours
Monday – Friday
10 am – 4 pm

Saturday & Sunday
10 am – 3 pm

Reservations
Not accepted

Cards
V, MC, Debit

Drinks
No alcoholic beverages

Takeout
Yes

Outdoor Dining
Patio

Website
No

Other Location

510 – 77 Avenue SE
(Calgary Farmers' Market)
403.991.6086

Galaxie Diner | Diner

BACK when there were only a few break-fast diners in Calgary, there would always be a lineup at the Galaxie on weekend mornings. (And at a few weekday lunches, too.) People loved the retro diner look, the compact surroundings and the to-heck-with-the-calories food. Then the breakfast market boomed with a passel of new bacon-and-egg joints filling the void. And the lineup at Galaxie? Still there.

Hard-core Galaxians wait for a table or booth to open up while those with less patience and greater hunger opt for the counter fronted by vinyl stools. There's only so long a person can linger in the doorway listening to the sizzle of bacon and breathing in the fresh coffee (though they'll pour you a cup of joe while you wait—that's nice).

It's not that the Galaxie staff are slow. They work that flat-top grill like a well-tuned fiddle, cranking out omelette after burrito, Benedicts after burgers. Yes, you can get a Galaxie Burger for breakfast. Why not? You can even get a Belmont Bleu Burger topped with Danish blue cheese and crisp bacon. (The Belmont is a good sister diner in Marda Loop, with a similar menu.)

There's also a Scramwich—a ham-and-cheese omelette folded onto grilled bread. Plus a heart-stopping Montreal smoked meat omelette—for $14.25, seven ounces of smoked meat is worked into an omelette along with sautéed onions, mushrooms and "plenty" of cheese. It comes with "endless toast." (And a resuscitator, perhaps?)

Address
1413 – 11 Street SW

Phone
403.228.0001

Hours
Monday – Friday
7 am – 3 pm

Saturday, Sunday &
Holidays
7 am – 4 pm

Reservations
Not accepted

Cards
V, MC, Debit

Drinks
No alcoholic beverages

Takeout
Yes

Outdoor Dining
No

Website
galaxiediner.com

Other Location

Belmont Diner
1, 2008 – 33 Avenue SW
403.242.6782
belmontdiner.ca

Giuseppe's

Italian Deli & Market

Address
1207 – 1 Street SW

Phone
403.232.6230

Hours
Monday – Friday
7:30 am – close

Saturday & Sunday
9:30 am – close

Reservations
Accepted

Cards
V, MC, AE, Debit

Drinks
Fully licensed
No corkage

Takeout
Yes

Outdoor Dining
No

Website
giuseppesitalianmarket.com

Step into Giuseppe's Italian Market at lunch and you'll be greeted by chaos. In a good way. In a way that smells like a busy Italian kitchen. A big wood-fired pizza oven sits centre stage with a sandwich and pasta station off to one side, a deli station behind it, and a coffee and dessert station near the front. There'll be lineups at each one and people milling in between. It's not immediately clear where to order or where to pay.

Here are a few possible strategies: Head for the station that smells the best or go to the one with the shortest lineup. Personally, I look for wherever chef Carmela Monna is cooking. I've loved her food for years, first at Lina's and then at Sal's. Her meatball sandwich is my standard for how a meatball sandwich should be—hot, thick, tasty meatballs bathed in a tangy tomato sauce on a crusty roll (no wearing white shirts here).

The pizzas are pretty decent, too—thin crusted, topped with your choices, quick-cooked in a smoking hot oven. And the pastas have been known to quell an appetite upon occasion. But I've never been big on their desserts—they are cold out of the fridge and seem somehow uninspired.

As for the chaos? If you don't feel *la dolce vita* after a few visits, try taking your lunch to the upstairs restaurant section. It doesn't open until 5 pm most days, and there'll be plenty of spots.

Graduate Foods

Pakistani & Indian

WHEN Shazia Naz and Mohammed Zia-ul-Haque moved to Black Diamond from Karachi via London a few years ago, they noticed a gap in the local culinary scene. There were no Indian or Pakistani restaurants for kilometres around.

So they decided to open one and call it Graduate Foods. They chose the name to indicate that this would be a place where even poor students could get a good meal for a good price.

Graduate Foods has only four tables, but that's OK because most of the orders are takeout. And even if you dine in at one of the sun-washed tables facing Main Street, your food will come in a takeout container.

There's an offering of four main courses—two vegetarian dishes (dal and a mixed vegetable curry) for $8 each and two meat dishes (butter chicken and beef curry) for $11 each. They come with either rice or nan, and you can mix them up a bit (beef curry, dal and rice, for example). There is also a handful of appetizers, including what they call a potato kebab, and it packs a punch. The ingredients for it and for the other "kebab" of mixed vegetables are puréed and then formed into patties and fried. Naz prepares the food the way she does at home, so the spice level is significant. I'd rate it at a pleasant medium that would, however, be way too hot for my mother.

I like Graduate Foods. It fills a big culinary gap in the Foothills.

Address
114 Centre Avenue W
Black Diamond

Phone
403.933.3320 ·

Hours
Tuesday – Saturday
11 am – 8 pm

Reservations
Accepted

Cards
V, MC, Debit

Drinks
No alcoholic beverages

Takeout
Yes

Outdoor Dining
No

Website
No

Han's | Taiwanese & Szechuan

THERE'S not a lot to Han's, a tiny cafe inside Chinatown's City Plaza: two short rows of tables seating about thirty, some grimy menus, the kitchen at the back. Tea comes in big glasses, and the washroom is outside in the food court. When the staff aren't working, they hang out in the front because there's nowhere else to hang out. It's the kind of place you might easily pass by.

But for hotheads who measure a good Asian restaurant by the amount of heat incorporated in the food, Han's is a gem. It hails from Szechuan and also from Taiwan, where the cuisine draws flavours from all over China. So some dishes here are very mild, but others can smoke your head off.

I, and seemingly many of Han's fans, like their forcefully flavoured dishes, such as the simply and aptly named "spicy chicken." It comes loaded with hot peppers. And garlic. And salt. Delicate, it is not. Forceful, it is. Same with the green beans, served compellingly tasty, laden as they are with ground pork and chopped, fried, heavily salted garlic. Great stuff.

But I am most impressed with the rice here. It's perfect. Steamed, with every grain plump and separate. No clumping, no hard bits, just high-quality rice expertly cooked.

I like the service, too—direct, prompt, to the point. The food arrives whenever it's ready, in whatever order it has been cooked. And did I mention that it can pack serious heat?

Address
303 Centre Street S
(City Plaza)

Phone
403.263.5667

Hours
Tuesday – Sunday
11 am – 8 pm

Reservations
Accepted

Cards
Cash only
ATM in City Plaza

Drinks
Beer only
Corkage $5 per bottle

Takeout
Yes
Delivery

Outdoor Dining
No

Website
No

Harvest

WITH its rustic wood floors, steaming mugs of java and coterie of dogs (outside) and babies (inside), Harvest typifies Canmore. It's a great place to catch up on where the best cross-country ski tracks are, whether the hiking trails are dry and clear, and who's heading up Ha Ling Peak on the weekend.

It's also likely the first place to have folks sitting outside on a sunny, late-winter afternoon. That's partly because the patio catches the sun nicely and partly because the crowd that gathers here is outdoorsy. It's a friendly, folksy and fun place. And the food is pretty good, too.

Harvest is run by a team of locals who enjoy their customers and who bake thick slabs of carrot cake, roll chipotle chicken wraps, and create big pots of tomato soup for a non-stop crowd of locals and tourists alike. The baking is always hearty and homespun, the wraps are creative and jump with fresh flavours, and the soups are just plain comfortable.

But keeping it in the Canmore family, the earnest group that owned Harvest from 2004 to 2011 (Mike and Misha Reed and Melanie Brehon) has moved on and passed the torch to a new earnest group (Jessie and Kurt Fonseca, Ryan Eckert and Hollie Kendal). The new owners have kept everything the same, right down to the chalkboard menu and the icing on the hot-to-go cinnamon buns.

And water bowls for the dogs. Gotta have those.

Address
718 – 10 Street
Canmore

Phone
403.678.3747

Hours
Monday – Saturday
10 am – 4 pm

Reservations
Not accepted

Cards
V, MC, Debit

Drinks
No alcoholic beverages

Takeout
Yes

Outdoor Dining
Deck

Website
No

Heritage Deli

Step up to the counter at Heritage Deli & Bakery and you'll be challenged to decide between a multitude of Eastern European delights. Perogies, cabbage rolls, garlic sausage, beet borscht, hunter's stew—decisions, decisions.

The solution? At least a partial one? Combo #1, a plate of four cheese-and-potato perogies, a cabbage roll, chunks of garlic sausage and a scoop of bacon-laden hunter's stew. You know there'll be a healthy dollop of sour cream, too. Did I mention this is a *lunch* combo? For $9? You won't go hungry here.

This is serious food, fuel for manual labour. Heritage Deli, one of Calgary's most popular Polish and Ukrainian delis, is packed with heavy, doughy, meaty things. Potato pancakes? Got 'em. Beef sausage rolls? You bet. Perogies to-go? How does eleven varieties sound? Then there are the cakes and pastries, the poppyseed strudel and the Polish cottage-cheese cake. It goes on and on.

Kathy Batorowska and her crew pinch 12,000 perogies a week! And they roll 1,200 to 1,500 cabbage rolls a day! And then there is Batorowska's father's recipe for garlic sausage. She can't even count how many rings of it she's made over the years.

Most orders are to-go, but there are twenty seats for dine-in. The tables fill and clear quickly during lunch hour.

And the beet borscht? You can get it with Combos #4 and #5 or by itself in four sizes, including extra-large.

Address
1912 – 37 Street SW

Phone
403.686.6835

Hours
Monday – Friday
9 am – 6 pm

Saturday
9 am – 5 pm

Reservations
Accepted

Cards
Debit

Drinks
No alcoholic beverages

Takeout
Yes
Delivery

Outdoor Dining
No

Website
heritagebakeryanddeli.ca

High Country Cafe

A TRIP into the Millarville area wouldn't be complete without a stop at the High Country Cafe for coffee and a slice of pie (preferably raisin). That is, unless it's breakfast time when a good old pile of bacon and eggs—pie, optional—is the way to go.

High Country Cafe is a local watering hole, a place to catch up on the goings-on in the area and to chew the fat, plus a bit of home cooking, with owners Dori and Gordie. The tiny, twenty-seat space is cosy, to say the least. There are a number of tables, but in reality, it's one big communal gab-fest. People stay awhile and enjoy the company along with the wall-to-wall collection of Western memorabilia.

Aside from the non-stop coffee, which is remarkably good, the cooks rustle up hamburgers, steaks, fish and chips, and other country diner fare. Simple stuff, prepared heartily and with care.

It's worth the stop at High Country for the outdoor ambience, too. The cafe looks like an old gas station and is set back from the highway enough to allow for loads of parking. And during the warmer months, there's a patio for another thirty-five customers. There's a great vista to the east for sunrises and, when traffic has died down, a serene quiet to the area. It's a little piece of Foothills' heaven within a half-hour of Calgary.

And, there's pie.

Address
Corner of
Highways 22 & 549
Millarville

Phone
403.931.3866

Hours
Tuesday – Friday
6 am – 3 pm

Saturday & Sunday
8 am – 3 pm

Reservations
Accepted

Cards
V, MC, Debit

Drinks
No alcoholic beverages

Takeout
Yes

Outdoor Dining
Patio

Website
No

The Himalayan

Nepalese

ASIDE from the big Sunday hotel/golf course brunch offerings, weekend lunch buffets can be difficult to find. Lunch buffets seem to fit best with the weekday office crowd that needs a quick fix tempered by enough variety to satisfy everyone in the group. But Sanjay Rajbhandari has bucked the trend successfully at The Himalayan with his weekday *and* weekend lunch buffet (it actually runs from Tuesday through Sunday) for a value-packed $12.50.

The Himalayan's buffet has the added advantage of introducing you to the delights of Nepalese cuisine. Perhaps you haven't had jomson-spiced vegetables or a stewy beef tekwa. These and other dishes are flavoured with the unique spices of Nepal. Some are spicy hot, taking influences from neighbouring India, while some are mild, hewing more to the southwest parts of China. Either way, the foods are uniquely Nepalese.

If you delve into the printed menu, you'll find other interesting and perhaps new words such as momo (dumplings), tarkari (a Nepalese curry) and chatamari (a Newari-style crepe—the Newa people being indigenous to Kathmandu). Interesting tastes, too. As for my favourites, there's the butter shrimp and the sweet bread (nan filled with sweet coconut). And the Nepalese staple of dal bhat (rice and lentils) served with various meats and/or vegetables.

Some dishes are over $15, so plan accordingly. A trip to The Himalayan is meant to take you up a mountain of flavour, not dollars.

Address
3218 – 17 Avenue SW

Phone
403.984.3384

Hours
Tuesday – Saturday
11:30 am – 2:30 pm

Sunday
Noon – 2 pm

Tuesday – Thursday &
Sunday
5 pm – 9 pm

Friday & Saturday
5 pm – 10 pm

Reservations
Recommended

Cards
V, MC, AE, Debit

Drinks
Fully licensed
Corkage $15 per bottle

Takeout
Yes
Delivery

Outdoor Dining
No

Website
himalayancuisine.ca

Holy Grill

Burgers & Paninis

Look behind the counter at the Holy Grill—under the stainless steel hood fan that has the menu scrawled on it—and you'll see a great big slicer. That's the epicentre, the holy grail, so to speak, of the Holy Grill.

I think if you took away any other aspect of this place—the seats, the hood fan, the grill itself—the Yee brothers who run the place would find a way to work around it. But without their slicer, how could they deal with the demand for their thin-sliced beet or sweet-potato chips? And how could they slice all the cold cuts for their paninis? They'd be hooped.

Sure, I could see the Yees—Jonathan, Andrew and Nick—telling people that their all-day breakfast was the way to go. "Have a Bacon-Avocado Crisp," they'd say. "Or a Pacific Benedict. It's two poached eggs, smoked salmon, spinach and hollandaise. It's great! Or how about a Sausage NicMuffin—Italian sausage, Cheddar and an egg on an English muffin? You don't need those beet chips today!"

They might be able to convince a few people to follow the breakfast route or to have one of their famed burgers or paninis. But without chips? There might be a riot. Regulars might tear the marble tiles from the walls, rip up the banquettes and write nasty slogans on the bright white walls.

But don't worry. That slicer is too heavy to be going anywhere.

Address
827 – 10 Avenue SW

Phone
403.261.9759

Hours
Monday – Friday
7:30 am – 4 pm

Saturday
10 am – 4 pm

Reservations
Not accepted

Cards
V, MC, AE, Debit

Drinks
Fully licensed
No corkage

Takeout
Yes
Delivery

Outdoor Dining
Patio

Website
holygrill.ca

Holy Smoke

Southern BBQ

WHAT can you say about a joint that offers less than a dozen menu items and still has folks lining up for lunch? I'd say they must know what they're doing.

Parked in a low building on Manhattan Road just off Blackfoot Trail, Holy Smoke is smellable from a kilometre away. Look for the big black smoker next to the building and the procession of burly guys heading inside to order pulled pork sandwiches and pieces of pecan pie.

Holy Smoke does slow-smoked Southern barbecue of pork shoulder, beef brisket, sausage and pork ribs. There's chili con carne and thick Brunswick stew, too, and sides of coleslaw, baked beans, potato salad and corn bread. It's simple, easy to order (at the counter) and mighty tasty. Don't be gettin' fussy—there ain't no substitutions or fancy accoutrements like plates. Most everything is served on paper-lined plastic trays, and the only cutlery is plastic.

In sauce, though, there's lots of variety. Look for the table topped with big sloppy bottles of house-made concoctions and help yourself. Then set yourself down at one of the four plastic-tableclothed tables and tuck in. Messy? You bet. But so, so good.

And enjoy the cheekiness of the surroundings—bathrooms labelled Jesus and Mary, a logo of a pig in a monk's robe and staff with nametags like Cooter or Daisy or Ten Gauge. And tuck your paper napkin into your shirt if you'd like. It's that kind of place.

Address
4, 4640 Manhattan Road SE

Phone
403.605.9365

Hours
Monday – Friday
10 am – 8 pm

Saturday
11 am – 4 pm

Reservations
Not accepted

Cards
V, MC, AE, Debit

Drinks
Beer only
Corkage upon request

Takeout
Yes

Outdoor Dining
Picnic tables

Website
holysmokebbq.ca

Istanbul

Turkish

As holes in the wall go, Istanbul Kebab House is a doozy. Stuffed into a dowdy strip mall between Chic N Sassy salon and the Leather Pocket billiard parlour, Istanbul doesn't exactly jump out at you. But pull into the mall's dusty lot around lunchtime and you'll be buffeted by the heady scents of organic chicken shawarma roasting on a rotisserie and lamb kebabs sizzling on a smoking grill.

Inside you'll find Nejim Ozkan, owner and chef of Istanbul, hard at work. He'll be mixing a white-bean salad of fresh tomatoes, parsley and sumac and dousing it with olive oil and lemon juice. He'll be deep-frying calamari and serving it with his own yogurt. He'll be topping pide—basically a Turkish flatbread— with mushrooms or feta or diced beef. And if your visit coincides with the lunch break for James Fowler High School across the street, he'll be serving a long line of students, too.

The Istanbul was a fixer-upper when Ozkan moved in a few years ago. Since then, he's redone the kitchen, laid new floor tiles, added fresh paint and worked the spot up into a hole in the wall. An overhead, back-lit menu describes the various dishes, and customers head to the counter to order.

In the evenings, the rack of lamb and eggplant baked with cheese are popular. That's when the dimmed lights and the scent of grilled lamb make Istanbul look less like a hole in the wall and more like a secret find.

Address
4129 – 4 Street NW

Phone
403.229.0542

Hours
Monday – Saturday
11 am – 9 pm

Reservations
Accepted

Cards
V, MC, Debit

Drinks
No alcoholic beverages

Takeout
Yes
Delivery

Outdoor Dining
No

Website
No

The Italian Store

Italian Cafe

THE Italian Store is so out of the way, tucked behind the big Canada Post sorting centre off McKnight Boulevard, you might think no one would go there. Wrong. The Italian Store carries a huge collection of Italian foods, many from its parent company Scarpone's, and it always seems to be packed—even though they doubled the size of the store a couple of years ago.

Off to one side of the retail area is a forty-seat Italian cafe run by a cadre of dedicated Italian cooks. Just follow your nose to the savoury scent of pizzas baking and sausages grilling or your ears to the sounds of customers revelling in the food. This is big Italian fare, well prepared and served at cheap prices. Everything is under $10, including the foot-long paninis at $6 each.

The porchetta, sitting in a glaze of gravy, is a popular lunch choice. And the pizzas, cooked in huge rectangular pans and sliced to order, disappear quickly. The lasagna and cannelloni, both heavily topped with thick tomato sauce, are scooped up for immediate consumption or plopped into containers for home consumption.

But I'm hooked on the calzones—huge, baked turnovers of dough packed with meat, cheese, roasted vegetables and sauce. Looking like a deflated football, a single calzone is a meal for two. But if you can eat the whole thing, the cooks will give you a big smile. And maybe a sweet, creamy cannoli.

Address
5140 Skyline Way NE

Phone
403.275.3300

Hours
Cafe:
Monday – Saturday
10:30 am – 3 pm

Store:
Monday – Saturday
9 am – 5 pm

Reservations
Accepted

Cards
V, MC, Debit

Drinks
No alcoholic beverages

Takeout
Yes
Delivery

Outdoor Dining
Patio

Website
No

Jimmy's A & A

Middle Eastern

THE undisputed king of shawarma, Jimmy Elrafih, knows a good thing when he sees it. He took his family's poky little Pleasant Heights corner store, with its small sideline of takeout shawarma, and turned it into a dining destination for fans who love donair and chicken shawarma. Where once sat racks of chips and cans of soup, there are now twelve—yes, twelve—upright rotisseries running half the length of the store, as well as a cooler stuffed with Middle Eastern delights like tabbouleh and baklava. (You can still buy some basic convenience items like milk, but not like before.)

Now, the scent of Jimmy's roasting meat and garlic wafting through the neighbourhood is enough to send arriving fanatics into paroxysms of joy. Stepping inside, that aroma is almost overwhelming. And intoxicating. You step up, order your shawarma and wait impatiently for it to be sliced, drizzled and folded into a pita with your choice of toppings.

Then the dilemma. Do you stand there gobbling up your shawarma, garlic sauce dripping down your arm, while those still waiting stare hungrily at your lunch? Do you step outside and brave the weather? Do you head to your car and eat while parked? Or while driving? (A big no-no.)

Or do you head home to your own table? Can you resist the temptation for that long? And just how will your house smell tomorrow if you break that beast out in the kitchen? It'll smell like Jimmy's, of course. Is that a bad thing?

Address
1401 – 20 Avenue NW

Phone
403.289.1400

Hours
Monday – Friday
9 am – 10 pm

Saturday
10 am – 10 pm

Sunday
10 am – 8 pm

Reservations
Not accepted
(No seating)

Cards
Debit
ATM

Drinks
No alcoholic beverages

Takeout
Yes
Delivery

Outdoor Dining
No

Website
jimmysAandA.com

Jonas' Restaurant

Hungarian

JONAS' Restaurant is an unknown spot that's always packed.

"Huh?" you think. "What's this guy talking about? That's an oxymoron if I've ever heard one."

For over ten years now, Janos and Rosza Jonas have served delicious Hungarian food in this long, narrow downtown restaurant. Often when I talk about it, people tell me they've never heard of the place, yet every time we go, it's chock full of customers. But it appears to be a regular clientele that adores the food.

So why don't others know about this gem? Is it that Jonas' is hidden under the facade of a big condominium building? Is it that Hungarian is just not a trendy food style? Is it that the Jonas' team spends time and effort on making customers happy instead of doing major promotions?

I don't know the answer, but I do know I like Jonas' bean goulash soup, their mushroom paprikash with nokedli (homemade dumplings) and their apricot palacsintas (crepes) for dessert. I also like that almost everything comes in two sizes so that Catherine can have a "small" (small? hah!) paprikash for $11.50 at lunch, $13 at dinner, and that I can have the "regular" (read: ginormous) serving of cabbage rolls or beef stew.

I like the tone of Jonas' too—its discreet, hidden location, the conspiratorial corners and the plethora of Hungarian decorations. Stepping into Jonas' is like finding a great cafe on the streets of Budapest, right down to Rozsa's professional and sassy service.

Address
937 – 6 Avenue SW

Phone
403.262.3302

Hours
Tuesday – Friday
11:30 am – 2 pm
5 pm – 9 pm

Saturday
5 pm – 9 pm

Reservations
Recommended

Cards
V, MC, AE, Debit

Drinks
Fully licensed
Corkage $10 per bottle

Takeout
Yes

Outdoor Dining
No

Website
jonasrestaurant.homestead.com

Joycee's | Caribbean

DOWN on the corner of Edmonton Trail and 1st Avenue NE, at the entrance to Bridgeland, there's a gas station and a strip mall that, by any estimation, are nondescript. But look closely and you'll see Joycee's Caribbean Foods, a bastion of jerk chicken, curried shrimp, goat roti and Jamaican patties.

Joycee's used to be Joy's, but Joy retired and Joycee took over. It's a happy coincidence of names. I'm sure infrequent visitors wouldn't notice a change; Joycee's continues both the Caribbean market that Joy started years ago as well as the takeout, or dine-in, hot dishes.

You order your food at the same counter where folks are purchasing their groceries, and then you wait. You might grab one of the seats that line the south-facing windows and enjoy a view of the gas pumps. You might wander the aisles and browse the cans of pigeon peas and bags of Irish moss algae. Or you might hang out at the counter and shoot the breeze with the staff and other customers.

Soon your order will come. Maybe a pound of jerk chicken—with extra sauce—to take home in a Styrofoam container. Maybe a curried chicken roti on a disposable plate to eat by the window. Maybe some Juici patties, brought in from Jamaica, to take-away or eat there.

Whatever you have, it will make you sit up and take notice. The food carries a full Island burn, making it the tangiest food in all of Bridgeland.

Address
5, 630 – 1 Avenue NE

Phone
403.234.9940

Hours
Tuesday – Saturday
10 am – 6 pm

Reservations
Not accepted

Cards
V, MC, Debit

Drinks
No alcoholic beverages

Takeout
Yes

Outdoor Dining
No

Website
No

Kabab Hut | Pakistani & Indian

I LIKE the look of Kabab Hut. It's open and fresh, with seating on the main floor and upstairs. There's a counter for ordering and a clear view into the kitchen so you can see—and smell—what's going on. And what's going on is some good Pakistani and Indian cooking.

There are kebabs, of course: seekh kebabs of ground, spiced chicken or beef cooked on skewers in a tandoor oven and chicken tikka, whole chunks of marinated chicken cooked in a similar way. Plus curries and biryanis, some being vegetarian, and a couple of Hakka-style dishes—chili shrimp and chili chicken. And sure, there's butter chicken, too, plus a bit more. Nothing unusual, but all prepared with flavourful intensity.

Kabab Hut is located in Calgary's curry belt of Westwinds and Falconridge and is surrounded by many similar places. Where it stands out is in the richness of its spicing, especially when matched with the prices. The meat for the seekh kebabs is firmly packed around the skewers and emerges from the tandoor with a smoky, spicy savouriness. The chicken tikka is tender and permeated with flavour. The channa (chickpeas) is creamy— maybe a touch too oily—but packed with well-balanced spices. And almost everything is under $10.

Service is quick and friendly at Kabab Hut. A cup of chai is offered while waiting for your order, even though the food arrives very quickly. It's a fine way to kick off a kebab feast.

Address
155, 5120 – 47 Street NE

Phone
403.590.7101

Hours
Monday – Friday
11 am – 11 pm

Saturday
Noon – 11 pm

Sunday
1 pm – 11 pm

Reservations
Accepted

Cards
V, MC, Debit

Drinks
No alcoholic beverages

Takeout
Yes
Delivery

Outdoor Dining
No

Website
No

Kaffee Stube | German

I'VE never seen as many kinds of mustard as they have at Edelweiss Village. There must be a couple of dozen. The jam selection is awesome, too. And the chocolate? Wow!

A quick stroll through the aisles of Calgary's most popular German deli reveals an amazing array of delicacies from Germany and other European countries. It's a brief diversion while waiting for my plate of frikadelle (a pork and beef patty) with German potato salad and sauerkraut ($11). I know I won't have to wait long because the frikadellen have been shaped and cooked and are waiting, bathed in gravy, for people like me to come along. It's already a big plate of food, but some folks upscale it with a bowl of pea soup or borscht or a side order of perogies or bratwurst. (Bratwurst is a side order? Don't you love this food culture?)

I just stick to my frikadelle plate, though, and slide into a table in Kaffee Stube, the sixty-five-seat dining area at Edelweiss. It's clean and flowery in a Black Forest way, well tended and packed with others enjoying a hearty German lunch. I'm being abstemious because I want a go at the pastry counter, maybe for a piece of cherry cheesecake or an apple strudel. The cakes and pastries look fabulous and are dwindling quickly, so I eat quicker. Decisions, decisions. OK, hazelnut torte it is. Mmmmm.

With a jar of Inglehoffer creamy dill mustard to-go.

Address
1921 – 20 Avenue NW
(Edelweiss Village)

Phone
403.282.6600

Hours
Monday – Wednesday
9:30 am – 6:30 pm

Thursday & Friday
9:30 am – 7:30 pm

Saturday
9 am – 5:30 pm

Reservations
Not accepted

Cards
V, MC, Debit

Drinks
No alcoholic beverages

Takeout
Yes

Outdoor Dining
No

Website
edelweissimports.com

Kaffir Lime

Indonesian

Considering Indonesia is the fourth most populous country in the world, you might think we'd have more of that country's food around these parts. There have been a couple of sit-down Indonesian restaurants here over the years, but all have passed away. Now, though, we're lucky to have a small Indonesian food kiosk called Kaffir Lime—named after the citrusy leaf used in Indonesian cuisine—in the Kingsland Farmers' Market.

Kaffir Lime is squeezed into a tiny space in the food-court area of Kingsland. There's enough room for a hot table filled with beef rendang, gado gado, lemon-grass chicken and such and a cold table laden with fresh vegetables. There's also enough room for the two staffers to work, so long as they don't move around too much. It's a charming space with some serious fare.

When you order, the chef assembles each dish from the food in front of him and adds the finishing touches—a sauce here, some herbs there. It's all very thoughtful.

Every bite speaks of the freshness and depth of Indonesian cuisine. The Indonesian slaw is layered with a fresh lemon-grass and herb-infused dressing. Coconut milk adds a creamy savouriness to the lemon-grass chicken, the rendang jumps with deep flavour and even the jasmine rice is tasty.

It somehow seems unfair to be chowing down on such complex, lush cuisine in a food court, but at the same time, it's a pleasure. Kaffir Lime deserves a larger forum. Perhaps one day it will get one.

Address
7711 Macleod Trail S
(Kingsland Farmers' Market)

Phone
403.852.7491

Hours
Thursday & Friday
9 am – 6 pm

Saturday
9 am – 5 pm

Sunday
10 am – 4 pm

Reservations
Not accepted
(Food-court seating)

Cards
Debit
ATM in market

Drinks
No alcoholic beverages

Takeout
Yes

Outdoor Dining
No

Website
No

Kawa

Espresso Bar

ON an early evening when most other coffee houses were quiet, we found a full house at Kawa Espresso Bar. A jazz trio was playing Hot Club music, and a multinational, multilingual crowd was enjoying food, wine, beer and more than a little coffee. There were all ages and looks, and to a person, everyone was having a good time.

Owners Les and Ottilia Jaworski had envisioned Kawa as an Eastern European-style coffee house that would be busy day and night. To achieve that, they started off brewing and pulling the best beans available and eventually introduced an international evening menu of items like bruschetta, salmon en papillote, a Western omelette sandwich and a bison-bean-chili dip. It's a short, diverse menu, and there's a breakfast one, too, plus a panini-quesadilla-style lunch one. They added an eclectic, intelligent wine list and an even longer, smarter and more popular beer menu. And they topped it all off with a non-stop list of live performances.

As for the food, our bastilla pie may not have been as crisp as some, but was honestly the tastiest we've had. Our Wiener schnitzel sandwich was excellent, too. We found out later that the bastilla was from Moroccan Castle (a good but non-Cheap Eats restaurant) and the schnitzel, from Vienna Lux (a place reviewed in this book). So some food is brought in, some is made in-house. Our finale, an in-house apple torte was fruity and fresh, perfect with an espresso.

Kawa does it all extremely well. No wonder the Jaworskis' dream has come true.

Address
101, 1333 – 8 Street SW

Phone
403.452.5233

Hours
Monday – Thursday
7 am – 11 pm

Friday
7 am – 2 am

Saturday
9 am – 2 am

Sunday
9 am – 9 pm

Reservations
Not accepted

Cards
V, MC, Debit

Drinks
Fully licensed
No corkage

Takeout
Yes

Outdoor Dining
Patio

Website
kawacalgary.ca

King's | Chinese & Western

Address
104 Meridian Road NE

Phone
403.272.2332

Hours
Monday – Friday
7:30 am – 4 pm

Saturday & Sunday
8 am – 2 pm

Reservations
Not accepted

Cards
V, Debit

Drinks
Beer only
No corkage

Takeout
Yes

Outdoor Dining
No

Website
kingsrestaurant.net

Before noon every day, King's parking lot is packed with wide-hipped half-tons and Audi coupes. More vehicles circle restlessly, hoping to find a spot. Inside, a lineup builds at the entrance as the hungry crowd in the already-full dining room waits for its fix.

A few of the assembled glance at the Chinese art on the tomato-soup walls, a brief distraction from their hunger. But their attention is quickly drawn to the front of the room. There, cooks slide blue-and-white ceramic bowls through a little pass-through window—the dishes sit on the sill momentarily, the aroma of their contents wafting forth. Soon, staff in red T-shirts swoop in to collect the bowls for speedy delivery. These are the objects of everyone's desire—King's wonton soup.

Most are King's original war wonton, a blend of meaty broth, barbecued pork, noodles and steamed vegetables. Others are variations, some with seafood, still others with no noodles or vegetables. All will include hand-formed wontons, plucked from the couple of thousand that King's staff make each day.

True, some folks come to King's for a good bacon-and-egg breakfast. Even devotees can have a hard time with wonton at 8 am. And some folks delve into that odd Prairie hybrid known as "Chinese and Western" cuisine, sharing clubhouse sandwiches and ginger pork.

But most folks just wait their turn, silently and impatiently, for their own bowl of made-to-order wonton.

Kinjo

STEP into either Kinjo location, and if you're lucky, you'll be attacked by a large man wielding a big knife. That man will be Peter Kinjo, owner, head sushi guy and mastermind behind two of the most popular sushi bars in the city. And yes, that knife will be sharp, so just do what he says and enjoy yourself.

If you're at the Macleod Trail location, grab a seat along the boat bar and help yourself to plates of sushi as they float by. Or order some tempura or teriyaki. If you go to the Dalhousie location, walk into the dining room through the big red gates, which Kinjo calls his "god gates." Here is where you can leave your troubles behind and let the staff treat you well. It's the same food at the same prices at both places; they just don't have a boat bar up north.

What they do have up north is a shiny new 1.5 million dollar renovation of what used to be a Kelsey's restaurant. Kinjo took it over and revamped it, and the result is a very pretty place that opened in early 2011, taking the northwest by storm and packing folks in regularly.

Happiness is at the core of Kinjo's restaurants. His staff sing songs and tell bad jokes and pass out free Pocky (a Japanese sweet) to everyone. It's lively and fun and quick. Even if you are attacked by a large man with a big knife.

Address
415, 5005 Dalhousie Drive NW

Phone
403.452.8389

Reservations
Accepted for groups of 8 or more

Outdoor Dining
Patio

Address
7101 Macleod Trail S

Phone
403.255.8998

Reservations
Not accepted

Outdoor Dining
No

Common Info

Hours
Daily
11 am – 10 pm

Cards
V, MC, AE, Debit
ATM

Drinks
Fully licensed
Corkage $10 per bottle

Takeout
Yes

Website
kinjosushiandgrill.com

Kol3 | Vietnamese Crepes

THE question I had when first entering Kol3 was not about their banh xeo (Vietnamese crepes), but rather, about where Kol1 and Kol2 were. The answer turned out to be simple: They don't exist. The young couple who own Kol3 have a son named Kole. They flipped the "e" in his name to a "3" and voila—Kol3 was born.

Now, back to those banh xeo. A few Vietnamese places make these rice-flour and turmeric crepes, but Kol3 decided to specialize in them. Theirs include coconut milk in the batter, and they prepare a half-dozen varieties, ranging from the traditional one loaded with shrimp, bean sprouts, mung beans, grilled onions and mushrooms with a choice of meats to a bacon-cheeseburger version filled with ground beef, cheese, bacon, onions, tomato and pickles and a breakfast one stuffed with bacon and eggs. They're plate- and stomach-filling servings for $11.50 and are sided with a salad plus a bowl of nuoc mam (fish sauce) for that sweet, vinegary bite. My traditional one was maybe a little heavy on bean sprouts for my taste, but I really liked the overall lightness, freshness and crispiness.

Kol3 also offers a few variations of pho (beef broth soups) and some spring and salad rolls in this cheery Kensington space. The walls are painted in bright pastels and chairs are plastic, but plans are to upgrade the look soon.

So, good effort at Kol3. Maybe someday there'll be a Kol4.

Address
24 – 12 Street NW

Phone
403.263.3666

Hours
Daily
11 am – 9 pm

Reservations
Accepted

Cards
V, MC, Debit

Drinks
No alcoholic beverages

Takeout
Yes

Outdoor Dining
Sidewalk patio

Website
kol3restaurant.com

La Belle Patate

Québécois Fast Food

When a courier arrives, the folks behind the counter at La Belle Patate are discussing the fattiness of the smoked meat being sliced. The courier offers a hearty "*Salut!*" as he drops a box of fresh cheese curds on the counter, and the conversation turns to last night's hockey game. Discussion revolves around the Habs' need for more scoring power. All of the above takes place in the French that was born in La Belle Province.

This tiny corner of Quebec is in the Elk Run Industrial Park of Canmore, Alberta, where views are of the Three Sisters, not Mount Royal. Inside, though, La Belle Patate is as Québécois as it comes—a welcome remembrance of home for the many Quebecers who live in the Bow Valley.

The smoked meat sandwiches are hot and juicy. The poutine, available in three sizes and many variations (all with the authentic and squeaky cheese curds) is as good as it gets. And the grilled hamburgers are a delight. Then there are the steamies (hot dogs) piled with house-made coleslaw, and they didn't forget the spruce beer either.

Former Montrealers John Lott and Tara Langlois opened La Belle Patate to satisfy their culinary longings of home and, in the process, have found a wealth of hungry fans—both Québécois and non-Québécois. They've created a warm and simple place that provides quick take-away meals or casual dine-in options.

And if you're a Habs fan, all the better.

Address
4, 102 Boulder Crescent
Canmore
(Elk Run Industrial Park)

Phone
403.678.0077

Hours
Tuesday – Saturday
11 am – 11 pm

Sunday
Noon – 9 pm

(Check for current hours)

Reservations
Not accepted

Cards
V, MC, Debit

Drinks
No alcoholic beverages

Takeout
Yes

Outdoor Dining
3 picnic tables

Website
No

La Cantina | Italian

QUESTION: Where can you have a great Italian meal and a game of bocce ball at the same time? Answer: At La Cantina in the Calgary Italian Club. And you don't even have to be a member.

La Cantina is truly a hidden culinary gem. It's the in-house cafe for the club, but because it belongs to a non-profit society, they can't advertise. On Saturdays and Sundays, it's reserved for private functions. The rest of the week, though, it's wide open for anyone—member or not.

So if you want simple, tasty food (Italian, of course) at prices that will make you reach for your glasses to make sure you haven't misread the menu, check out La Cantina. You can order a good veal parmigiana ($12), some hand-rolled gnocchi Romano ($14), veal and pork lasagna ($13) or a wild-mushroom risotto ($15). And maybe a bottle of Pasqua primitivo ($28) or a Chianti Ruffino ($34). The food is robust and well prepared (it is the Italian Club, after all), the service is delightful and the wine is plentiful.

La Cantina has an Italian sports-bar tone with red-checkered tablecloths, multiple televisions, sports photos and memorabilia dotting the walls, and five lanes for bocce along the length of the cafe. A group of us booked the lanes for an after-dinner tourney one wintery evening and had a blast. They may not post our photos on the wall, but we'll be back for more. (BTW, guess who won?)

Address
416 – 1 Avenue NE
(Calgary Italian Club)

Phone
403.264.2032

Hours
Monday – Friday
11 am – 2 pm
5 pm – close

Saturday & Sunday
Private functions only

Reservations
Recommended

Cards
V, MC, Debit

Drinks
Fully licensed
No corkage

Takeout
Yes

Outdoor Dining
No

Website
calgaryitalianclub.com

Lazy Loaf & Kettle

Bakery Cafe

WE all have certain food rituals such as always eating the peas last or always buying Twizzlers when grocery shopping. One of my rituals involves stuffing a turkey—when I am about to do so, I invariably head over to the Lazy Loaf & Kettle for a loaf or two of their Kettle Bread.

This bread is dense and grainy (nine grains and no fat, eggs or dairy) and makes the best stuffing ever. It is also the foundation of fine—and huge—sandwiches at the Lazy Loaf, whether layered with deli meats or tuna salad or just cheese and tomato. They present you with a long list of additional ingredients from which to choose, so a sandwich here becomes your own creation.

The KB is baked every day—any leftovers end up in a day-old discount bin at one side of the cafe. That's where I look first for my turkey bread. If there's none there, I order up a fresh loaf or two at the counter.

Then I stand in line to pay with all the other hungry souls. We slowly meander past the big slabs of Nanaimo bars, cinnamon buns and other cakey delights, and I'm usually tempted to pick up a sweet, too. (That's wily marketing!) And since I have dessert, I might as well order a sandwich. And maybe a bowl of soup. And then, why not an espresso?

That turkey can wait.

Address
8 Parkdale Crescent NW

Phone
403.270.7810

Hours
Monday – Friday
7 am – 9 pm

Saturday & Sunday
8 am – 9 pm

Reservations
Not accepted

Cards
V, MC, AE, Debit

Drinks
Fully licensed
No corkage

Takeout
Yes

Outdoor Dining
Patio

Website
lazyloafandkettle.com

Lighthouse Cafe | Seafood

WHEN you're out food shopping, do you ever feel like chowing down on those purchases right now? (After they're prepped, I mean.) Happens to us a lot.

Usually, we have to head home and get cooking. But if you're at Billingsgate Seafood Market, you can do your shopping and eat it too. That's because Billingsgate has a tidy little thirty-two-seat cafe right in the market.

As you might suspect, most of what the Lighthouse Cafe offers revolves around seafood—cod and chips, grilled steelhead trout, oyster burgers, clam chowder, crab cakes, that sort of thing. About the only items sans seafood are Caesar salad, coleslaw and fries. But if you're in Billingsgate, you're likely a seafood lover, so that's fine.

On my last visit, I had a bowl of lobster bisque for $6—creamy and lobstery but a touch too salty—and a halibut burger for $8. The "patty" was actually a piece of breaded halibut, crisp and hot from the fryer, slathered with tartar sauce and piled into a fresh bun. It was great. Of course, I had the halibut with a side of fries: huge, thick potato slices, again crisp and almost too hot to eat. Good chips, and I appreciate that they keep the malt vinegar on the table at all times. Smart.

I also like that they offer to cook any fresh seafood you see in the Billingsgate display case. That's perfect for those of us who just can't wait.

Address
1941 Uxbridge Drive NW
(Stadium Shopping Centre)

Phone
403.269.3474

Hours
Saturday – Wednesday
11 am – 6 pm

Thursday & Friday
11 am – 8 pm

Reservations
Accepted

Cards
V, MC, Debit

Drinks
Beer & wine only
No corkage

Takeout
Yes

Outdoor Dining
No

Website
billingsgate.com

Lina's | Cappuccino Bar

LINA's Cappuccino Bar was never meant to be so popular. When Lina's Italian Market opened way back in 1995, the bar was a simple adjunct to a store filled with Italian cold cuts, pastas and cheese. Back then, it literally was a "cappuccino bar" with a few pastries and a couple of hot lunch dishes.

But it quickly became a focal point for the business. Folks would come in, shop a bit and then settle into the little cafe for lunch and coffee. They stayed, they ate, they lingered. Lina's staff would whip up more hot specials, which would be gone quickly. The individual pizzas were popular and so were the combos of pasta and sausage or veal.

So when Lina moved her place into bigger digs in 2001, the cappuccino bar expanded to over fifty seats and the kitchen more than doubled in size. Now to get lunch, you have to stroll by the pastry section, the pizzas, the hot table, the panini case and, finally, the espresso machine before you place your order with the staff. Let's see how your resolve holds up under that kind of assault.

The prices have stayed remarkably low. The pizzas and panini ring in at $6 to $7 each, and the hot plate combos are under $10. And the servings are far from skimpy. This is quality food served in abundance.

Lina's is a taste of Italy served fresh and hot. No wonder it's popular.

Address
2202 Centre Street N

Phone
403.277.9166

Hours
Monday – Friday
9 am – 7 pm

Saturday & Sunday
9 am – 5 pm

Reservations
Not accepted

Cards
V, MC, Debit

Drinks
Fully licensed
No corkage

Takeout
Yes

Outdoor Dining
No

Website
linasmarket.com

Lion's Den

Diner

WHEN I wrote about Lion's Den a few years ago in my last *Cheap Eats* book, I mentioned that they might not be around much longer. But Lion's Den seems to have better staying power than a bad cologne. (I mean that in a good way.) In spite of all the demolition and construction around them, Lion's Den soldiers on. Happily, it's still open for breakfast, lunch and dinner seven days a week.

And a visit here is still an experience. You'll be subjected to owner Rico Festa's stories and jokes and to Rose Festa's wonderful cooking. She whips up a great clubhouse sandwich, and as I've said many times, could give lessons on how to make french fries. (Hand cut, crisp, hot, terrific!)

Lion's Den is an original diner, replete with regulars, a long counter, a big milkshake machine and a hypnotically eclectic collection of art on the walls, including a couple of vintage velvet paintings. You can slide into a real Naugahyde-covered booth or twirl on a stool at the counter. You can try to hide at one of the free-standing tables, but Rico will search you out to tell you a story or two.

The location makes Lion's Den a perfect diversion when heading to or from the Stampede Grounds. Maybe a pizza before a Flames game, a slab of lasagna before a concert or a piece of pie after an event to let the traffic die down.

For as long as it lasts. I hope that's a lot longer.

Address
234 – 17 Avenue SE

Phone
403.265.8482

Hours
Daily
9 am – 9 pm

Reservations
Accepted

Cards
V, MC, AE

Drinks
Fully licensed
No corkage

Takeout
Yes

Outdoor Dining
No

Website
No

Little Chef | Upscale Family Dining

IF you saw kids in pyjamas toddling into a restaurant, you'd probably wonder if you were in the right place. If it's the Little Chef, though, jammies are just a small indication of how homey the restaurant is and how comfortable customers are in going there.

Arthur Raynor and his crew run what Raynor calls an "upscale family restaurant," serving an extended family of regulars who have been coming for years. Customers step in, say a quick hello to the staff (likely Raynor's wife or daughter), settle in at a favourite table and order a favourite item like fish and chips, an omelette or a grilled cheese sandwich. Or they might glance at the weekly specials listed on the chalkboard, which could be chili with garlic toast or a lamb burger or a piece of grilled salmon. And there will always be liver and onions, even if you don't see it listed. Just ask. Liver aficionados give the Little Chef's liver high marks.

There will always be pies, too—steak and kidney, steak and mushroom, and chicken—served with fries, mashed potatoes or salad for $12. Raynor shows his British roots in these pies: great pastry, tender meats and delicate seasonings. They're also available to take home and bake yourself for $7.25.

And yes, there may well be kids there in their jammies, enjoying their favourite dish at their favourite table. Nice to be a regular at the age of three.

Address
*555 Strathcona Boulevard SW
(Strathcona Square
Shopping Centre)*

Phone
403.242.7219

Hours
Monday
11 am – 3 pm

Tuesday – Friday
11 am – 8 pm

Saturday
9 am – 8 pm

Sunday
9 am – 3 pm

Reservations
Recommended

Cards
V, MC, Debit

Drinks
Fully licensed
No corkage

Takeout
Yes

Outdoor Dining
Patio

Website
No

Little Lebanon

Lebanese

WHEN Valentine's Day last rolled around, we dropped into a little 17th Avenue place for a quiet dinner for two. Our budget—$25, all in. And Little Lebanon was the spot.

But before you call for reservations (they don't actually take them), be aware that Little Lebanon does the fast-food version of Lebanese food. So here's the decor: fluorescent lighting, an overhead menu, red cafeteria trays and a half-dozen stools for dining at the counter. Romantic? Maybe not. Fast and tasty? Yes, sir.

They do a different spin on the pita sandwich here. You can get your fillings the usual way, wrapped in nice pita bread, or you can have it folded into fresh dough, which is then baked in a huge conveyor-belt oven. In just two minutes, you'll have a hot, crisp pocket loaded with your choice of beef donair, chicken shawarma or chickpea falafel, plus all the trimmings and garlicky sauces. (Don't be breathing on anyone besides your valentine after a visit here.)

The salads and dips are great, too. The fattoush has crisp pita chips and a tart pomegranate dressing. The tabbouleh has a fine balance of parsley and bulgur, and the hummus is creamy and lemony.

The owners are charming and hospitable, passing out fatayer (stuffed, freshly baked pastry triangles) and/or baklava (crunchy, not too sweet) to diners. And offering quick, cheap meals of good food.

All in, $23 for us. And home by 7 pm with $2 to spare. Great stuff.

Address
3515 – 17 Avenue SW

Phone
403.217.0500

Hours
Monday – Friday
9 am – 9 pm

Saturday
9 am – 8 pm

Sunday
9:30 am – 6 pm

Reservations
Not accepted

Cards
V, MC, Debit

Drinks
No alcoholic beverages

Takeout
Yes

Outdoor Dining
No

Website
No

Lloyd's Patty Plus

Jamaican Patties

SOMETIMES I just feel like a spicy Jamaican patty. (Yeah, yeah, sometimes I look like one too.) And when I do, there's no place better than Lloyd's Patty Plus to add some spice to my life. Lloyd ("Just call me Lloyd," he says) has been making patties in Calgary since 1984 when he opened Lloyd's Caribbean Bakery a few blocks away from what is now Lloyd's Patty Plus.

The current place is mostly a wholesale bakery where Lloyd bakes patties and Jamaican breads that go to big stores such as Sobey's and to food distributors like Cysco. But in the front end of the bakery, there is a small (as in, ten seats) eat-in space. Because, as with most baking, you can't beat a fresh patty hot out of the oven. Lloyd does a lively to-go business, too.

He makes five kinds of patties for $2.25 each. Buy more than two and that price drops to $2 each. He's got chicken and beef in regular or spicy modes (the spicy ones aren't going to induce sweat) and vegetarian in regular only. The pastry is flaky and yellow with turmeric, and the meat fillings are saucy and flavourful. My suggestion is to start with a vegetarian patty for your appetizer and move on to a spicy chicken or beef one for your main course. Two patties will satisfy most people.

There may be nothing here for dessert, but hey, you've only spent $4.50.

Address
202, 255 – 28 Street SE

Phone
403.207.4455

Hours
Monday – Saturday
8 am – 6 pm

Reservations
Not accepted

Cards
Debit

Drinks
No alcoholic beverages

Takeout
Yes

Outdoor Dining
No

Website
No

The Loop

Breakfast House

ARRIVE at The Loop on a weekend morning around 8:30 and the place will likely be quiet. You'll have your choice of tables. But drop in a half-hour later and you may be hard-pressed to find a seat. Seems 9 am is the breakfast time of choice for weekend Loopers. (Note: "Loop" refers to the Marda Loop neighbourhood in which The Loop resides.)

That flood of breakfasters continues unabated until well into the afternoon as an all-age crowd congregates here. The volume goes up and the coffee goes down as orders of bacon and eggs and grilled pancakes land on tables. The staff move quickly about the room, aware that coffee is a prerequisite and that the morning meal should not be far behind. It's an efficient ballet of movement as servers slide between tables, taking orders, dropping off plates of eggs Benedict, pouring more coffee and readying seats for the next hungry customers.

The Loop flips some of the best pancakes in the city, straight up or peppered with fruits. These cakes are big, thick and buttermilky and served with a small pot of warmed maple syrup (nice touch). They also come with a sincere side of fruit—pieces that are large, fresh and varied, not just limp, throwaway orange slices.

And when Catherine orders her bacon crisp, it comes out crisp, which keeps her happy. That's a good thing, too. You don't want to mess with her bacon.

Address
2015 – 33 Avenue SW

Phone
403.802.2174

Hours
Monday – Friday
7 am – 3 pm

Saturday & Sunday
8 am – 4 pm

Reservations
Monday – Thursday only

Cards
V, MC, AE, Debit

Drinks
Fully licensed
No corkage

Takeout
Monday – Friday only

Outdoor Dining
Patio

Website
theloopbreakfasthouse.ca

Luxor | Egyptian

DASH off the train, quickly grab something to eat, jump on the next train. That's what I call LRT dining, and there aren't a lot of good options out there for it.

Happily, though, Luxor is one. Located near the west end of the downtown LRT, Luxor is Calgary's sole Egyptian culinary outpost. If we could have only one Egyptian restaurant, Luxor is a good one to have. It's large and lively, packed with fresh Egyptian food and music and friendly staff.

Luxor always smells so good. The aroma is a combo of grilled meats and crisp scents of lemon, cumin, coriander and other spices. I like that it's not too heavy on the garlic. Make no mistake, garlic and onions are present, but they don't seem as overpowering as at some Middle Eastern places.

There are loads of vegetarian options in Egyptian food and great salads like tabbouleh or fattoush. A real treat at Luxor is the chickpea salad. It's loaded with peppers, cucumbers, tomatoes, chickpeas and mint, all doused with a lemony, mouth-puckering dressing. Or the eggplant dip called baba ghannouj, perhaps the best version in town.

And how can you resist the Mummy Wrap of spicy chicken folded into a pita with turnip and cucumber pickles, fresh tomatoes and lettuce, all drenched in the creamy, spicy house dressing? Or a pizza (yep, pizza) topped with red peppers, feta and spinach?

It's all enough to make you miss your train. But you don't have to.

Address
937 – 7 Avenue SW

Phone
403.282.0030

Hours
Monday – Saturday
7 am – 10 pm

Reservations
Accepted

Cards
V, MC, Debit

Drinks
No alcoholic beverages

Takeout
Yes

Outdoor Dining
No

Website
No

Magic Bowl | Chinese (Cantonese)

I'VE largely been off Cantonese buffets and dim sum dishes lately. It has to do with the number of places that bring in prepackaged, frozen foods from fast-food factories around the city—the food from these places can be bland and oily and often all tastes the same. But not every Chinese restaurant does this. There are many good ones that make their food in-house, places like the Magic Bowl.

Owned by a Guangzhou-born couple who also took their culinary training there, the Magic Bowl handcrafts all their dim sum. The shrimp dumplings are packed with crustaceans, rolled in rice dough and steamed to a tender, tasty perfection. The pork and chive dumplings are equally good, rolled, wrapped and steamed just the way they should be. (The work that must go into these helps me understand why many restaurateurs outsource.) At lunch, each dim sum order is only $3.50; there's a limited selection at dinner for $4.50 each.

The dim sum and other menu items epitomize the elegant, sublime food of Canton, handcrafted to bring out the simple, natural flavours. For more intensity, the Magic Bowl includes some dishes, such as Szechuan beef and Shanghai-style spareribs, drawn from the spicier areas of China.

The Magic Bowl is all of twenty-eight seats, with little for decor. That's OK—it's all about the quality of the food. Which is more than enough to bring me back.

Address
12, 1215 Lake Sylvan Drive SE

Phone
403.271.9366

Hours
Monday, Wednesday & Thursday
11 am – 2 pm
4 pm – 10 pm

Friday
11 am – 2 pm
4 pm – 11 pm

Saturday
11 am – 3 pm
4 pm – 11 pm

Sunday
11 am – 3 pm
4 pm – 9 pm

Reservations
Accepted

Cards
V, MC, Debit

Drinks
Fully licensed
Free corkage

Takeout
Yes
Delivery

Outdoor Dining
No

Website
magic-bowl.com

The Main Dish

IT's one of those weeks—you're working too many hours, there's nothing in the fridge and you don't have the energy to shop or plan meals. Sound familiar? That's where The Main Dish comes in.

Saunter into their Bridgeland shop and dinner can be figured out in, say, less than a minute. It could be as simple as buying a block of chilled Mac and Cheese or a rack of sauced ribs to pop in the microwave. Or, if your energy is on the rise, you could go more of the cooking route with fresh sausages and pasta, some tomato sauce and a chunk of cheese. Or you could just chow down on whatever The Main Dish's chefs have that's hot and ready, maybe a sun-dried tomato and turkey meat loaf or a seafood arrabbiata pappardelle.

And what about the morning? You could stop by for an omelette or some hot quinoa porridge and a blast of espresso.

Whatever the time of day, The Main Dish has you covered. It's a well-executed concept for dine-in, take-home or cook-yourself options. It's not a huge place, but each item seems thoughtful, like it's something you'd actually want to eat. Part healthy (like lentils or chickpea and feta salad), part decadent (say, butter chicken or coq au vin), The Main Dish is the kind of place you won't leave hungry or empty handed.

For southerners, there's now a kiosk in the relocated Calgary Farmers' Market, too.

Address
903 General Avenue NE

Phone
403.265.3474

Hours
Monday – Friday
7 am – 10 pm

Saturday
8 am – 10 pm

Sunday
9 am – 9 pm

Reservations
Not accepted

Cards
V, MC, AE, Debit

Drinks
Fully licensed
No corkage

Takeout
Yes

Outdoor Dining
Patio

Website
tmdish.com

Other Location

510 – 77 Avenue SE
(Calgary Farmers' Market)
No phone

Mirch Masala

ACROSS 36th Street from Sunridge Mall, there's a strip mall with a very good Indian restaurant called Mirch Masala. Run by Surjeet (Sam) and Charanjit (Rampi) Thind, Mirch Masala has all of twenty-two seats and a menu that ranges from cauliflower pakoras and potatoes with onion gravy to fish tikka and lobster masala. It's a pretty place done in bright reds and yellows with Indian wall decorations and glass-topped tables. What it doesn't have is a buffet.

What they offer instead are combo plates of a meat or vegetarian dish such as butter chicken or lamb curry or spiced lentils served with a vegetable korma, rice and nan for $9. That's a great deal. You can super-size your combo with a second meat or veg dish for only $10, all in. And this is good food. Sam learned the kitchen trade at Rajdoot when it was one of the best Indian restaurants in town. He uses good ingredients and prepares them in a simple, forceful Northern Indian style. The combo plates are big with the takeout crowd.

For dining in (or more takeout), there's also the full menu of six different styles of curry, seven biryanis, seven kinds of Indian bread and more—a lot of variety for such a small place. And very high quality for the price. Few options are over $13. There's always the lobster masala, too, but that's $35—fodder for a different book.

(By the time you read this, there should be a second, larger location nearby—this one with a liquor license.)

Address
3, 3735 Rundlehorn Drive NE

Phone
403.568.9994

Hours
Monday – Friday
11 am – 9 pm

Saturday
Noon – 9 pm

Reservations
Accepted

Cards
V, MC, AE, Debit

Drinks
No alcoholic beverages

Takeout
Yes

Outdoor Dining
No

Website
No

Other Location

3, 6208 Rundlehorn Drive NE
403.293.7440

Mirchi

MIRCHI is a place for those who just can't get enough flavour in their food. Every bite of an Afghani tikka—charbroiled chicken breast lacquered with a yogurt-peppercorn sauce—or the daily dal will have your taste buds dancing for joy. (It may open a few facial pores, too.) And if that's still not enough, tuck into a Mirchi kebab, a spicy minced beef kebab that is purported to have "more kick than a Bollywood hero."

The original Mirchi on 12th Avenue is a tiny, sixteen-seat wonder. Slide in past the two slim rows of tables, join the line and peruse the overhead menu. Or just go with whatever is on the hot table that day—it'll be good, I promise. And if they have the goat chops available, check them out. Best goat chops I've ever had. (Admittedly, there aren't a lot of goat chops around these parts.)

And now there's a second Mirchi—a larger downtown spot where the Sahara restaurant used to be. This one is licensed. Ordering off the menu here can get a touch pricey, but their lunch buffet is only $14. Still a bargain, and if you're a sheesha fan, they've got a separate room for that, too.

Purists seem to prefer the charm of the too-hot, too-cold, too-drafty character at the 12th Avenue Beltline Mirchi. It's a simple concept that works extremely well. But both locations pack more flavour per dollar than practically any others in town.

Address
825 – 12 Avenue SW

Phone
403.245.3663

Hours
Monday – Thursday
11:30 am – 10 pm

Friday
11:30 am – 11 pm

Saturday
1 pm – 11 pm

Sunday
3 pm – 9:30 pm

Reservations
Accepted for groups of
5 or more

Cards
V, MC, Debit

Drinks
No alcoholic beverages

Takeout
Yes

Outdoor Dining
No

Website
mirchirest.com

Other Location

739 – 2 Avenue SW
403.262.7222

Mission Diner

Diner

THERE'S a restaurant revival going on in the Mission district along 4th Street SW. Fuze has arrived in the old 4 St. Rose location, Wurst is in the process of reviving memories of Franzl's Gasthaus and Mission Diner has moved in where a Nellie's location used to be.

Mission Diner has kept Nellie's tradition of breakfast. Owner Mhairi (pronounced VAH-ree) O'Donnell knows that the morning crowd needs its fix of pancakes and eggs, of good coffee and a friendly setting. So she scrubbed and sanded and repainted everything that didn't move (she used to own a house-painting business) and opened Mission Diner in early 2011. I'll bet some sleepy-eyed regulars have yet to realize the change. The place still has character (read: old and small), but it looks better than it has in years.

Mission Diner is quick on the draw with the coffee pot—a requirement for a good diner. The 15 Kilo java, locally roasted by a spinoff of Phil & Sebastian Coffee Roasters, is poured with a smile, too—another requisite. Food-wise, there's a bunch of straight-ahead morning fare: eggs and bacon, omelettes, pancakes, sausages and such.

Mission has started doing evenings, too, with choices like meat loaf and burgers, all available with wine or beer or even shooters if you want. Nothing pushes the envelope, but everything is prepared to order and comes out hot and fresh.

That's the kind of revival that's welcome anywhere.

Address
2308 – 4 Street SW

Phone
403.453.0330

Hours
Monday – Thursday
7 am – 9 pm

Friday
7 am – 10 pm

Saturday
7:30 am – 10 pm

Sunday
7:30 am – 9 pm

Reservations
Accepted

Cards
V, MC, AE, Debit

Drinks
Fully Licensed
No corkage

Takeout
Yes

Outdoor Dining
No

Website
missiondiner.com

Momo Sushi | Japanese

THERE'S a small space on Macleod Trail across from Chinook Centre that ought to be a good location for a restaurant. Just look at the traffic generated by Chinook. Problem is, most of the traffic is heading straight to Chinook—it's not looking east across Macleod.

Too bad, because loads of folks have missed a couple of good restaurants (Praga Cafe and Mediterranean Grill) that have come and gone from this spot. But now there's a new tenant called Momo Sushi. If anything can get that traffic to turn east instead of west, it's sushi.

Momo comes to town from Vancouver, where there are two outlets. So they have experience. And it shows. Momo gave the room a full Japanese makeover with delicate rice-paper window coverings and a big sushi bar at one end. And they've gone with a straightforward list of sushi, sashimi, tempura, teriyaki, donburi and such.

I haven't gotten past the sushi yet, but what I've had has been good. It's all made to order, so the tempura shrimp at the centre of the dynamite roll is still warm when it's served. The rolls are tight and firm, and the rice is delicate and lightly sweet. The nigiri is huge, with large pieces of fish draped over the rice cakes. So you get a big hit of fish with each piece.

But it's still small on the pocketbook. I've had a simple sushi lunch here for under $10. Now if that doesn't stop traffic, I don't know what will.

Address
108, 6008 Macleod Trail S

Phone
403.457.2602

Hours
Monday – Friday
11:30 am – 2:30 pm
4:30 pm – 10 pm

Saturday, Sunday &
Holidays
11:30 am – 10 pm

Reservations
Not accepted

Cards
V, MC, Debit

Drinks
Fully licensed
No corkage

Takeout
Yes

Outdoor Dining
No

Website
lovemomosushi.com

Myhre's Deli

WHEN the lineup grew too long at Galaxie Diner, owner Brad Myhre had a unique solution—open another place next door. He called this one Palace of Eats after the downtown Calgary lunch counter that served patrons from 1918 to 1964. The new Palace of Eats was a stand-up joint, literally—there were no seats. It was busy, and it turned out that customers wanted to sit and linger, too. So after a while, Myhre added booths and mahogany wall panelling salvaged from the original Palace and renamed the spot Myhre's Deli.

The main food ingredient at Myhre's is Montreal smoked meat, brought in from Quebec Smoked Meat. Steamed and machine cut (hand cut on request), the meat is layered onto rye with a choice of mustards and served with coleslaw, a kosher dill and Old Dutch potato chips. Available in three sizes or as a Reuben with sauerkraut, it makes a great sandwich.

Myhre's does a few other sandwiches, too—bagel and lox, roast turkey, grilled tuna, pesto chicken, grilled cheese—and steamed, all-beef Nathan's hot dogs (*oui, un steamé aussi*, with homemade coleslaw). And that's about it.

In reality, they probably need little more than the smoked meat. That's what almost everyone orders. A smoked meat sandwich, a kosher dill and a bottle of black-cherry cola and you're in a little piece of Montreal heaven.

So you don't have to wait in line at Galaxie to get your food fix, unless you want to (it's good, too).

Address
1411 – 1 Street SW

Phone
403.244.6602

Hours
Monday – Friday
11 am – 7 pm

Saturday & Sunday
11 am – 4 pm

Reservations
Not accepted

Cards
V, MC, Debit

Drinks
No alcoholic beverages

Takeout
Yes

Outdoor Dining
No

Website
myhresdeli.ca

Nem Delight | Vietnamese

FOR over twenty years, Saigon was my favourite Vietnamese restaurant. But since the owners sold it in 2009, I've been looking for a new go-to place. And maybe, just maybe, I've found it. It's Nem Delight, which opened in Deer Run in early 2011.

I'm quick to jump on the Nem bandwagon because Kader and Thu La, the former owners of Saigon, are the ones who've opened it, along with their niece Cam Do. Trained at both Saigon and at SAIT, Do is a talented young chef.

Nem, named after a Vietnamese word for "rolls," does takeout only, but is packed with all the dishes that Saigon once did. There are the cha gio, or imperial rolls, of chopped chicken and vegetables all rolled in rice wrappers and then deep-fried. (They're still the best cha gio in town.) There are also the salad rolls with shrimp, chicken or beef, big bowls of bun and pho, Vietnamese subs, bubble tea and more. Many of the dishes are immortalized in large, glossy photos mounted on the walls. Staff skilfully pack everything for you to take home, ensuring wet ingredients don't make the dry ones soggy in transit. It works remarkably well.

One of the few shortcomings of Saigon was that they didn't have a lot of choice for desserts. But with Do's training, Nem offers caramel coconut flan, fried bananas and crepes filled with creamed berries or peaches.

So yes, perhaps a new favourite in the making.

Address
13750 Bow Bottom Trail SE
(Deer Valley Station)

Phone
403.235.5757

Hours
Tuesday – Sunday
11 am – 9 pm

Reservations
Not accepted
(No seating)

Cards
V, MC, Debit

Drinks
No alcoholic beverages

Takeout
Yes
Delivery

Outdoor Dining
No

Website
nemdelight.com

Odyssey

Family Dining

IF you want to avoid the dinner rush at Odyssey Pizza, Steakhouse & Lounge, you have two choices: go early or go late. When I say early, I mean around 4:30 pm or so. As for late, that's 7 pm or after. Between about 5 pm and 7 pm, you might be lucky enough to score a table, but don't hold your breath.

Odyssey is the destination of choice for those who like veal cutlets, chicken cordon bleu, $20-ten-ounce New York steaks and baked liver, each served on a huge platter with accompaniments like baked potatoes, vegetables and garlic toast. We're talking about serious amounts of food here, enough for lunch the next day.

A while back, when I put out a call to *Herald* readers for a good plate of liver and onions, I received a swack of suggestions. But the name that popped up most often, and with the grandest accolades, was Odyssey. So I went. Excellent service, friendly folks, tons of food and really fine liver—breaded lightly and baked. And for $12, we're talking about great food in great volume for a great price.

Odyssey does a brisk pizza trade, too—it's the thick, heavily loaded Greek style. Someday I may actually have one. If I can get past the liver, that is. How about if they did a liver and onion pizza? I'd be down for that.

Address
3814 Bow Trail SW

Phone
403.246.8889
403.246.8896

Hours
Monday – Saturday
11 am – 11 pm

Sunday & Holidays
4 pm – 8 pm

Reservations
Recommended

Cards
V, MC, AE, Debit

Drinks
Fully licensed
No corkage

Takeout
Yes
Delivery

Outdoor Dining
No

Website
odysseypizza.ca

Overeasy Breakfast

Diner

OVEREASY Breakfast. The name should be a tip that there could be eggs on the menu. Think that and you'd be right about this Edmonton Trail diner.

Located just a short stroll north of the iconic Diner Deluxe, Overeasy used to be Country Kitchen. But it's been renovated to include a banquette along one wall, a long table down the middle of the room and an open kitchen in the back. Funky wallpaper covers the walls and a kind of blackboard effect has been used on the ceiling. The chairs—re-padded and re-painted—are the only holdovers from Country Kitchen. Overeasy is a bright, cheery place that stops just short of being garish.

And it does breakfast and lunch all day—heavy on the breakfast. Eggs any way you want, with the usual meaty suspects or poached into four styles of Benedict or whipped into omelettes or crepes. They even do an Eggstra-Ordinary Brioche Sandwich that looks a lot like an open-faced Denver, albeit on brioche instead of toast. Plus a few pastas, burgers and sandwiches like the double-smoked BLT or the chicken club, both on brioche, too.

The ingredients are high quality, the fruit garnishes are actual sides rather than sad little melon slices and the coffee is good and quick, served by friendly staff. Overeasy isn't breaking any new ground, just 2,200 eggs a week. But they do it well. They're carving out a tasty niche in the growing breakfast-diner category, one egg at a time.

Address
824 Edmonton Trail NE

Phone
403.278.3447

Hours
Daily
7 am – 3 pm

Reservations
Not accepted

Cards
V, MC, AE, Debit

Drinks
Fully licensed
No corkage

Takeout
Yes

Outdoor Dining
No

Website
overeasybreakfast.com

Owl St. Kitchen

Modern Comfort

THE inimitable—and talented—Shelley Robinson is at it again. It seems that running the bucolic Baker Creek Bistro on the road to Lake Louise is just not enough for her. So, in the winter of 2010/11, she opened not one but two new places in Banff. One is the deli named Feast (see the "More Markets" section of this book), the other is the quaintly named Owl St. Kitchen.

Located in Banff's industrial area—between the Trans-Canada and Banff Avenue off Compound Road—Owl St. Kitchen is parked in a small spot on, yes, Owl Street. Mostly a takeout place heavy on daily specials, it seats about six inside.

It's the kind of place I always hope to find in light industrial areas. But it often seems I find soggy egg-salad sandwiches and week-old muffins instead. At Owl St., though, everything is fresh daily, from porchetta sandwiches and bison meat loaf to banana bread and fruit-filled scones. A pulled chicken sandwich that I tried, with its crisp bacon, toasted pecans and creamy mayo, was outstanding, and that banana bread is in a class of its own.

Many ingredients are sourced locally, so you may find a daily butternut-squash soup with sage brown butter or elk and deer salami or more bison in a bolognese sauce. Add in a wealth of other baking (cupcakes, cookies, sausage rolls), daily features that include chili and stew, breakfast specials and fair-trade coffee and there's nothing the least bit industrial about the food.

Address
6, 100 Owl Street
(Industrial Compound)
Banff

Phone
403.762.1008

Hours
Monday – Friday
8 am – 4 pm

Reservations
Not accepted

Cards
V, MC, Debit

Drinks
No alcoholic beverages

Takeout
Yes

Outdoor Dining
Small patio

Website
No

Pad Thai | Thai

BANFF Avenue is packed with restaurants big and small, pricey and cheap, excellent and mediocre. But one that stands out for offering quality and value in the most understated way is Pad Thai.

Located on the lower level of the Clock Tower Mall, Pad Thai is easy to miss. Even on the sunniest days, it's dim in that area. Pad Thai has added more tables in the concourse over the years, which has bumped up the seating to almost forty, but it's still a pretty discreet place.

This is the kind of spot where you'll find locals enjoying pork-filled dumplings and Thai green curries that are flavoured with coconut milk and packed with vegetables and chicken, beef or tofu. Folks are getting a good, inexpensive fix of fine Thai food. Some of them have been to Thailand and are trying to replicate their meals there. They'll have better luck here than anywhere else in the Rockies.

At Pad Thai, the hot dishes are hot, the mild ones, mild. But if you want more heat, just ask. Milder? They will do that, too. The restaurant may be small in size, but the chef/co-owner Khampiene Gran-Ruaz is large on ability. Red and Massaman curries join her green ones, and there is a long list of Thai appetizers, noodles, soups and stir-fries to keep your taste buds busy.

Note: The owners have a second larger and more expensive restaurant in Canmore called Thai Pagoda.

Address
110 Banff Avenue
(Lower Level, Clock Tower Mall)
Banff

Phone
403.762.4911

Hours
Daily
11:30 am – 9 pm

Reservations
Accepted

Cards
V, MC, Debit
ATM in mall

Drinks
Fully licensed
Corkage $10 per bottle

Takeout
Yes

Outdoor Dining
No

Website
No

Other Location

Thai Pagoda
1306 Bow Valley Trail
Canmore
403.609.8090

Pâtisserie du Soleil

Casual French Bistro

Searching for a good petit déjeuner or boeuf bourguignon in the southwest? If you're in the community of Woodbine, or anywhere nearby, you'll be happy to hear that Pâtisserie du Soleil has opened in what used to be a Dairy Queen at the west end of Woodbine Square. Why happy? Because it's good.

Pâtisserie du Soleil isn't exactly new though. There's been one in Glenmore Landing for over a decade. But that one is just for buying nice pastries and cakes and such. There's no dine-in option.

But the Woodbine location, opened in 2010, has thirty-two seats. Nice comfortable seats, at that. You still order DQ-style at the counter, but they've done some decent renos on the interior. And with the original floor-to-ceiling windows, it's an open, airy, comfy place to have coffee after a stroll through Fish Creek Park or to rendezvous with a business colleague for a casual repast.

But be forewarned: All the croissants and scones and breads are baked on-site. So any resolve to have just a coffee may melt quickly under the waft of fresh-baked pains au chocolat and beignets. And the cheesy croque monsieurs and the toasty banana bread French toast? They may just keep you there all day.

By the way, that croque monsieur, with a salad, is $9, and the steak frites is the priciest item at $14. And, they are making their own gelato, too.

So visit sunny Woodbine and let the *soleil* shine in through those big windows.

Address
2525 Woodview Drive SW
(Woodbine Square)

Phone
403.452.8833

Hours
Monday – Saturday
7 am – 8 pm

Sunday
7 am – 4 pm

(Check for extended summer hours)

Reservations
Recommended, especially weekends

Cards
V, MC, Debit

Drinks
Fully licensed
Corkage $10 per bottle

Takeout
Yes

Outdoor Dining
Patio

Website
patisseriedusoleil.com

Other Location

Bakery Only
1600 – 90 Avenue SW
(Glenmore Landing)
403.259.5864

Peppino

J OE Lecce and his team at Peppino have been perfecting the Italian submarine sandwich since 1993. And I think they've got it right. From the artichoke-turkey version to the Vesuvius (a tonsil-tingling blend of spicy salami and banana peppers), there are twenty-six meaty varieties from which to choose, plus nine vegetarian options like eggplant parmigiana or grilled red peppers. The subs are big, they're tasty, they're quick, they're fresh and they top out at $9. Like I say, I think they've got it right.

Some day I may finish working my way through the entire menu. But it's usually a toss-up between Joe's Special of mortadella, capicollo, and Calabrese salami with cheese, lettuce and the house Italian dressing or the classic Hot Italian Meatball sandwich, which as it says, is hot and Italian. (There's a nice little zip to the spicing on that one.) So I'm not making much headway.

Peppino is one of the most comfortable cafes in the Kensington area. It's a community hangout where people gather to discuss the issues of the day and where many neighbourhood workers grab a quick lunch or coffee. And on a sunny day, the south-facing patio is a warm and relaxing place to knock back your sub. It's a simple, pleasant, real place where everyone is welcome.

And if you want to make your own Italian subs at home, they'll happily sell you all the ingredients. But it's hard to beat all those years of perfection.

Address
1240 Kensington Road NW

Phone
403.283.5350

Hours
Monday – Friday
8 am – 6 pm

Saturday
10 am – 5 pm

Reservations
Not accepted

Cards
V, MC

Drinks
No alcoholic beverages

Takeout
Yes

Outdoor Dining
Patio

Website
peppinogourmet.com

Pfanntastic Pannenkoek

Dutch Pancakes

CALGARY'S a pancake town, no doubt about it. Any Stampede morning, a good layer of pancakes and maple syrup in the stomach is essential for a fine day of Stampeding. Any other time of year, too, pancake houses are busy with folks getting their flapjack fixes.

So it was only natural that the Pfanntastic Pannenkoek Haus (PPH), with its savoury and sweet Dutch pancakes, would be embraced by locals when it opened in 1995. Sure, people looked at their first thin, twelve-inch pannenkoek (maybe a shredded potato, onion and cheese one or a bacon and mushroom combo) and thought, "Well, that looks different." But heck, a pancake is a pancake in any language and in they dove. And they liked them.

So the PPH has become an institution, popular enough to have lineups on the sidewalk some weekend mornings. Once hooked, loyal pannenkoekers return frequently for one of the over seventy versions available, almost all of which are under $10.

For the multitude of variations—think mandarin oranges, ice cream and whipped cream sided with orange liqueur in a chocolate cup, or smoked sausage, leeks, mushrooms and cheese topped with salad as just two possibilities—I go for the simple ones. Like the lemon juice and brown sugar or the bacon and egg or the basic one drizzled with stroop—the thick, sweet Dutch syrup.

And I really like that I don't have to squeeze on my old cowboy boots to enjoy any of them.

Address
2439 – 54 Avenue SW

Phone
403.243.7757

Hours
Wednesday – Friday
9 am – 8 pm

Saturday
8 am – 8 pm

Sunday
8 am – 3 pm

Reservations
Accepted all day
Wednesday – Friday
& Saturday after 3 pm

Cards
V, MC, AE, Debit

Drinks
Fully licensed
No corkage

Takeout
Yes

Outdoor Dining
No

Website
dutchpancakes.ca

Phil & Sebastian

WHEN Phil Robertson and Sebastian Sztabzyb landed at the Calgary Farmers' Market in 2007, they were a couple of over-caffeinated, lapsed engineers who had a quest to bring a high-end coffee business to Calgary. They'd spent a lot of time learning the business and honing their craft in the coffee meccas of Portland and Seattle. And they wanted to bring their own version of West Coast coffee culture to Cowtown.

Their coffee-house gamble quickly paid off. As soon as local coffee geeks sniffed their first cup of P & S espresso, the lineups formed. But the shop was only open market hours, Friday through Sunday, not nearly enough for serious coffee aficionados.

Soon P & S started roasting their own beans and then launched an open-every-day cafe in Marda Loop. A second one in Chinook Centre soon followed. (And their market kiosk closed when the Calgary Farmers' Market relocated.)

With the new cafes, they started offering food and decided to keep things simple, local and fresh. They source from local producers such as Sylvan Star Cheese, Highwood Crossing, Winter's Turkeys and Broxburn Vegetables. They bring in pastries from Manuel Latruwe and breads and scones from Sidewalk Citizen Bakery. They cook up lamb confit sandwiches and vegetable soups and toss salads with grape-seed oil and balsamic vinegar. They offer daily specials and keep prices as low as possible.

And it works. In a few short years, Phil and Sebastian have become part of Calgary's culinary lexicon.

Address
2043 – 33 Avenue SW

Phone
403.686.1221

Hours
Monday – Friday
6:30 am – 9 pm

Saturday
7:30 am – 9 pm

Sunday
7:30 am – 5 pm

Outdoor Dining
Sidewalk seating

Address
6455 Macleod Trail S
(Chinook Centre)

Phone
403.255.4900

Hours
Monday – Friday
7 am – 9 pm

Saturday
7:30 am – 9 pm

Sunday
9 am – 6 pm

Outdoor Dining
Patio

Common Info

Reservations
Not accepted

Cards
V, MC, Debit

Drinks
No alcoholic beverages

Website
philsebastian.com

Pho Binh Minh

THEY'VE spiffed up Pho Binh Minh recently. There are new granite-topped tables and black-padded chairs. But don't think they've gone fancy or anything. It's still one of the scruffier places in this book. But for my dollar, it serves one of the best phos in the city.

Pho is a Vietnamese beef noodle soup, served here in sixteen different versions (and three different sizes of each version). There's the satay beef noodle soup and the beef balls noodle soup and the medium-rare beef, brisket, tendon and tripe noodle soup. You get the picture. (There's even a beef noodle soup filled with chicken.)

I usually go for the simple medium-rare beef noodle soup without any of the extra body parts. And I order the small portion, which is really enough for two. The extra-large could feed a big, hungry family. The soup is composed of a great beef stock (chefs everywhere, take note—this is how beef stock should taste), a swack of vermicelli noodles and loads of medium-rare beef slices, and there's a plate of fresh stuff on the side— bean sprouts, basil, lime wedges, chilies and a few things I don't recognize. I toss in whichever I feel like and add some seasoning from the assorted table condiments. This is a good bowl of soup and calls for both a spoon and chopsticks as well as a hearty appetite.

There's nothing delicate or polite about eating it, though. Best advice I can give? Wear black.

Address
4710 – 17 Avenue SE

Phone
403.235.2521

Hours
Sunday – Thursday
9 am – 9 pm

Friday & Saturday
9 am – 10 pm

Reservations
Accepted

Cards
V, MC, AE, Debit

Drinks
Beer only
Free corkage

Takeout
Yes

Outdoor Dining
No

Website
No

Pies Plus

CERTAIN culinary prognosticators south of the border predicted that pie would be one of the hot food trends of 2011. But for Patrick Cousineau and his team at Pies Plus, pie has been hot for over twenty years.

Cousineau, a second-generation pie man who took over the business from his parents, has a long list of popular pies to prove it—over eighty fruit or cream pies, plus an additional four meat ones and six quiches. Each day, he bakes a collection culled from that list—maybe blueberry-cherry and apple-raisin plus butterscotch cream and the always popular pecan. He'll have some whole ones freshly baked to take home for dinner, others sliced for immediate in-cafe consumption and many, many more in the freezer to "take and bake" yourself. ("Sure this pie is homemade," you can say. "I took it out of the oven an hour ago.") Whatever way you get it, it's always good—handmade with lots of filling, a flaky crust and not too much sugar.

The "plus" in the Pies Plus name refers to the light meals of quiche and soup or salads and sandwiches or beef stew or chili. You know . . . the preamble to the pie. Those items are pretty good, too, but it's still the pies that drive people to Pies Plus.

It's always been thus, prognosticators or not. Pies Plus customers have always been ahead of the curve.

Address
12445 Lake Fraser Drive SE
(Avenida Village)

Phone
403.271.6616

Hours
Tuesday – Saturday
8 am – 6 pm

Reservations
Not accepted

Cards
Cash & cheques only

Drinks
No alcoholic beverages

Takeout
Yes

Outdoor Dining
Sidewalk patio

Website
piespluscafe.com

Railway | Continental Cafe

HARRY and Daniela Griesser have made a big name for themselves as the go-to folks for Thanksgiving and Christmas turduckens. The couple can debone and stuff a duck into a chicken and then into a turkey faster than practically anyone in the business. (They did 360 of these deboned triple-headers for Christmas 2010.)

But let's not lose sight of the fact that they also run one of the slickest cafes in the Bow Valley. Their rotisserie (they were rotisserizing long before it became so popular) spins out chickens every day. A half chicken with fries or salad is $15, and it is glorious. Sandwiches are custom-built and served with soup or salad. And burgers—like curry chicken, beef with bacon, bison with goat cheese, elk with mushrooms—are tossed on the grill with regularity. Breakfast is served all day long, and there's a decent list of desserts that includes apple strudel and lemon cake.

It all sounds kinda fancy, doesn't it? But the Railway Restaurant, as opposed to the attached Railway Deli where you can stock up for the trail, is basically an upscale cafeteria: Step in, grab a tray, move along the line, order your meal and grab a seat. Except this is unlike any cafeteria of my memory. This one has excellent food—fresh, hot and nothing over $15.

There's even a single serving of what they call turducken pie. Mmmm—pastry with all that meat! Now that's my kind of cafeteria.

Address
101, 702 Bow Valley Trail
Canmore

Phone
403.678.3637

Hours
Restaurant:
Daily
11 am – 4 pm

(Call for extended summer hours)

Deli:
Daily
9 am – 7 pm

Reservations
Not accepted

Cards
V, MC, Debit
ATM

Drinks
Fully licensed
Corkage $15 per bottle

Takeout
Yes

Outdoor Dining
Patio

Website
railwaydeli.com

Raj Palace

Indian (Southern)

CRUISE through your typical Sunday buffet brunch and you'll find hot trays of eggs Benedict, sausages, pancakes and other breakfast fare supplemented by an eclectic mix of lasagna, ginger beef and barbecued chicken. Usually there's a big hunk of beef shining under a hot lamp at the end of the line, too.

But head downtown to Raj Palace on a Sunday and you'll find none of that. Sure, there'll be a buffet, but it will be stocked with dosas (crisp rice-lentil crepes filled with potatoes and other vegetables), vadas (thick chili-filled donuts), vegetable korma (a creamy curry) and a wealth of other lentil, chickpea and vegetable dishes. See, Sunday brunch ($13) at Raj Palace is dedicated to South Indian vegetarian cuisine. Much of this food, especially the rice and potato dishes, can be quite mild. But some is spiked with the lively presence of chilies. If Sunday morning is a little early in the week for that, there are bowls of yogurt to help douse the fire.

The rest of the week, the lunch and dinner buffets ($14) are still South Indian, but they're packed with meat and seafood dishes such as chicken tikka and lamb jalfrazi and fish curry. (And likely butter chicken.) In addition, you can order both meaty and vegetarian dishes off the menu.

But come Sunday, Raj Palace is all vegetarian and all buffet. There will be no hunk of beef in sight.

Address
731 – 6 Avenue SW

Phone
403.205.3672

Hours
Monday – Saturday
11 am – 2:30 pm
5 pm – 9:30 pm

Sunday
10 am – 3 pm

Reservations
Recommended

Cards
V, MC, AE, Debit

Drinks
Fully licensed
No corkage

Takeout
Yes
Delivery

Outdoor Dining
No

Website
rajpalace.ca

Red's Diner

Diner

Fine as 4th Street SW is for lunch and dinner choices, breakfast options have been a bit sparse. But the situation improved when Red's Diner opened recently in the former Charlebois fur shop just north of 17th Avenue. They do breakfast all day long, every day (plus lunch after 11 am).

And they do a diner breakfast the way it should be done—bacon, sausage, eggs any way you want them. (Go ahead, challenge the chef with, say, eggs poached lightly in espresso or scrambled with sardines, walnuts and jalapenos. Bet they'd do it. Not sure I'd want to eat it, but you might.) Buttermilk buckwheat pancakes, vegan quinoa with roasted almonds and pumpkin seeds, waffles, short-rib hash and eggs—there, that sounds a bit better doesn't it?

Red's looks the diner part, too, in a contemporary way. First off, look for the big pink-and-blue couch sculpture out front. Inside, there's a long, sleek counter with twirly stools and simple tables dotted around the room.

The staff are serious about getting you your coffee. Red's straddles the traditions of 1950's diners and the sensibility of today's customers. Want an espresso? (Without eggs?) No problem. A milkshake or float? Can be done, even with a shot of Jack Daniel's. A veggie burger? You bet. Poutine? *Bien sûr.* And if all you want is a straight-up BLT or a hot beef sandwich with homemade gravy, it'll be up in just a sec, hon, and with your choice of bread.

Address
1415 – 4 Street SW

Phone
403.266.3448

Hours
Daily
7 am – 4 pm

Reservations
Not accepted

Cards
V, MC, AE, Debit

Drinks
Fully licensed
No corkage

Takeout
Yes

Outdoor Dining
No

Website
redsdiner.com

The Rock | French-Asian Fusion

THERE used to be a Newfoundland pub in Calgary called The Rock. This Rock is not that Rock.

This Rock is an eclectic restaurant in an obscure location. The strip mall in which it resides is home to a number of restaurants (including Taketomi Village, which also appears in this book), but most of those eateries offer the cuisines of individual cultures. The Rock is different. The owner calls his food French-Asian fusion, and his cuisine seems more likely to be located at a downtown or Beltline address.

Be that as it may, the lower rent allows The Rock to produce very high quality food for a good price. A lamb burger with applewood-smoked Cheddar and fries or salad, for example, is $12, and tempura cod and chips is $10. An eight-ounce Sterling Silver sirloin is $18, and roasted duck breast with sautéed spinach and mushrooms and an orange-brandy sauce is $24. (I know those last two are getting beyond our budget, but I thought you'd like to know anyway. Plus, they come with your choice of two sides.)

This is very skilful food. The chicken-corn chowder ($6) is a silky velouté that had me scraping my bowl. And a shrimp burger on rice patties (with salad, $12) was outstanding. Messy to pick up because the rice patties tended to fall apart, but really tasty.

The Rock is simple and clean and pleasantly staffed. And as I said, it's eclectic. I like that.

Address
140, 920 – 36 Street NE

Phone
403.454.0242

Hours
Monday – Saturday
8 am – 9 pm

Reservations
Accepted

Cards
Debit

Drinks
Fully licensed
No corkage

Takeout
Yes

Outdoor Dining
No

Website
therockcalgary.com

Rocky's Burgers

THE last time I popped over to Rocky's Burgers, it was -23°C. The ketchup squeeze bottle sitting on the table at the side of the bus had an ice crust clogging its top and the vinegar looked pretty frosty, too. Rocky's picnic tables and wooden benches were abandoned and even the ever-present ground squirrels had taken the day off.

But one after another they came: a crew cab filled with overalled guys, a Mercedes SUV carrying two suits, an old Toyota holding a young couple and half-ton after half-ton half-hidden by white exhaust. Damn the weather—these people needed their Rocky burgers.

Frozen occupants ran quickly to the side window of the old Calgary Transit bus, placed their orders, paid and ran back to their still-running vehicles. And they waited.

Inside the bus, Rocky and his crew toiled over the grill. There, it was only marginally cooler than on a hot summer day. Burgers hit the grill, onion rings and fries sizzled in oil, and the whir of the milkshake machine filled the air.

One order done, an arm extended from the bus window into the chill air, the fist clutching a brown paper bag. "Number 30," the voice behind the arm hollered. A vehicle door opened and someone lunged to the bus, grabbing the bag. A splurt of frosty ketchup and the customer headed back to the car, smiling. Winter be damned.

Burgers

Address
4645 – 12 Street SE

Phone
403.243.0405

Hours
Monday – Friday
10 am – 3 pm

(Also open Saturday
10 am – 3 pm in
spring/summer)

Reservations
Not accepted
(No indoor seating)

Cards
Debit

Drinks
No alcoholic beverages

Takeout
Yes

Outdoor Dining
4 benches
5 picnic tables

Website
No

Ruby's Kitchen

Indian (East African)

F you're looking for an obscure, out-of-the-way joint that serves unique food, you might want to pop into Ruby's Kitchen in the Interpacific Business Park. Ruby Rayani cooks up a style of Indian cuisine that originated in India's Gujarat region, evolved in East Africa and has now made its way to northeast Calgary.

Ruby has some serious culinary skills. Raised in a restaurant family in Kenya, she says she cooks the same way for her customers as she does for her family. So as at home, her menu is not identical every day. There might be kuku paka, a chicken curry blended with creamed coconut, and a masala salmon, the fish and some potatoes coated in a thick and spicy tomato sauce. There might also be mandazi, the chewy, fried dough Ruby calls "Indian donuts," as well as kachori, her crisp chickpea-battered mashed potato and vegetable balls. The flavours are rich and robust but tempered by coconut, tamarind, yogurt and a variety of chutneys.

If you're lucky, you might find a spot at one of the few tables Ruby has in her cafe. Mostly, though, Ruby does takeout—but she has enough space in the back of her strip-mall bay to include a cooking school. So if you want to try your hand at this kind of cuisine, Ruby will teach you the tricks of her trade. (She'll even come to your home to teach.)

So drop in on Ruby some day. She's always looking for new family members.

Address
325, 3132 – 26 Street NE

Phone
403.452.7965

Hours
Tuesday – Saturday
11 am – 6:30 pm

Reservations
Not accepted

Cards
V, MC, AE, Debit

Drinks
No alcoholic beverages

Takeout
Yes

Outdoor Dining
No

Website
rubyskitchen.com

Rustic Sourdough Deli

German Deli

Rustic Sourdough Deli is in the east part of the building that houses Rustic Sourdough Bakery, a lively German bakery on 17th Avenue. The deli is the quieter space that, oddly, many folks—even a few who shop at the bakery—don't know about. But step into the deli and smell the soup. (Just don't stand there too long—folks behind you are hungry!)

The deli is about take-away soup and sandwiches. And about pairing them in ethereal combinations seldom replicated elsewhere. Think about a bowl of corn chowder, thick with corn, potato and smoked chicken, matched up with a grilled Reuben of Montreal smoked meat, sauerkraut, cheese and mustard on fresh rye bread. Is there anything better? And for $9, is there anywhere that offers such high quality and quantity with such a low price? The sandwich is huge and the soup, delicious.

On any given day, Rustic will have a couple of fresh-made soups, plus a daunting list of ingredients to layer into a sandwich. You can select from forty cheeses, eighty deli meats, a boggling array of vegetables and condiments, and a list of breads. (You know the bread will be fresh.) Or, you can choose one of the set-piece sandwiches like the Monte Cristo or the tuna melt. Tough choices.

And if you feel like dessert from the bakery side, well, you know that's going to be good, too. (FYI, the bakery also operates at the Kingsland Farmers' Market.)

Address
1305 – 17 Avenue SW

Phone
403.245.2616

Hours
Tuesday – Friday
8 am – 6 pm

Saturday
7 am – 5 pm

Reservations
Not accepted

Cards
V, MC, Debit

Drinks
No alcoholic beverages

Takeout
Yes

Outdoor Dining
No

Website
rusticsourdoughbakery.ca

Other Location

Bakery Only
7711 Macleod Trail S
(Kingsland Famers' Market)
No phone

Saigon Gourmet | Vietnamese

PEOPLE I always listen to: my wife, my mother, my haircutter. So when Sherry (the lady who cuts my hair) told me that she'd enjoyed really good food at Saigon Gourmet, I went right over. It helped that the restaurant is in the same Lynnwood strip mall as her salon.

And I've been back again and find Saigon Gourmet to be a pleasant, clean, cheerful place that serves a long list of familiar Vietnamese dishes—lemon-grass chicken, shrimp paste on vermicelli, big bowls of beef pho soup and so on. They're all good, served hot and fresh and in super-filling portions.

They do a few unique items, too, like the thin, steamed vermicelli patties. These are pretty much what they sound like—thin pucks of noodles that are steamed. They are then laid in a bowl to form the base of a dish that is topped with grilled shrimp or spring rolls or other good things. They're tasty-chewy and a different take on the food, a bit like a bowl of bun without the liquid. At about $11, they're also among the priciest things on the menu, but worth every penny.

Saigon Gourmet offers some of the best value and flavour combinations in town. For $7 to $10, you can get a fine meal of lively, lovely food. And it's not that heavy on fat. So you don't need to feel too badly about how much you've eaten.

At least that's what my wife says. And my mother. And Sherry.

Address
1603 – 62 Avenue SE

Phone
403.279.7447

Hours
Monday – Saturday
11 am – 9 pm

Reservations
Recommended for
large groups

Cards
V, MC, Debit

Drinks
Beer only
No corkage

Takeout
Yes

Outdoor Dining
No

Website
No

St. James Corner

Upscale Pub

FIRST things first: For the grammarians and Guinness purists out there, yes, perhaps it should be spelled St. James's Corner. Either way, after a few pints, it's not easy to say.

St. James Corner cooks up an immense menu of global pub food—nachos, pizzas, fajitas, burgers, beef dips, fish and chips, lasagna, Irish boxties, bangers and mash, shepherd's pie, lamb shanks and wings done ten different ways. And there's an additional list of brunch-ish things. So this is a very busy and ambitious kitchen. More importantly, they have eighteen brews on tap and a whole swack more by the bottle.

St. James does the pub thing well, from the airy, two-storey room filled with wooden furniture to the brisk and smiling service. The pulls are fast and frosty—so hopefully you like your beer on the chilly side.

But back to the food. Again adhering to pub tradition, it is some of the hottest I've been served around town. A bowl of clam chowder was creamy good and still almost too hot to eat by the time I finished it. Likewise the chicken pot pie—hot and good. More of a chicken stew with a puff pastry lid than a true pie, it was still tasty.

So St. James is a welcome addition to the revitalization of 1st Street SW—a friendly neighbourhood pub with decent food and good beer.

Address
1219 – 1 Street SW

Phone
403.262.1157

Hours
Monday – Wednesday
11 am – 1 am

Thursday & Friday
11 am – 2 am

Saturday
10 am – 2 am

Sunday
10 am – midnight

Reservations
Accepted

Cards
V, MC, AE, Debit
ATM

Drinks
Fully licensed
No corkage

Takeout
Yes

Outdoor Dining
Patio

Website
stjamescorner.ca

Schooner's Pub

How to build a better burger:

1. Start with a decent meat patty. (If you don't want to deal with forming your own, buy some top-grade commercial patties. Meat companies are making some pretty decent ones these days.) Grill the patty and add on a hearty slice of quality Cheddar.
2. Sauté onions, mushrooms and green peppers until they're lightly caramelized but still a little crunchy.
3. Have a good bun—not too big, not too small—and make sure it's fresh. Give it a sincere coating of barbecue sauce.
4. Assemble all of the above and add on three slices of perfectly crisp bacon.
5. Voilà, a burger with taste, texture and an overall yum factor.

And so it goes at Schooner's. It's as if someone actually understands how a burger should be constructed in order to maximize the strength of its elements.

Schooner's is that kind of thoughtful neighbourhood pub. The barkeep has one eye on the room, the other on the door. When regulars arrive, they're met with a warm welcome and a cold beer delivered to their favourite table before they've even sat down. And the server—young, pierced, black-clad—has a kind word and a smile for everyone. Now that's service.

So, good burgers, cold beer, warm welcome. Great pub.

Address
6416 Old Banff Coach Road SW

Phone
403.240.2424

Hours
Daily
10 am – 2 am

Reservations
Accepted

Cards
V, MC, AE, Debit
ATM

Drinks
Fully licensed
No corkage

Takeout
Yes

Outdoor Dining
Patio

Website
schoonerspub.com

South Fork | Home Cooking

THE hot hamburger sandwich sits lacquered under a patent-leather coat of gravy. The snow-white bread beneath slowly soaks up the gravy as I cut gently into the meaty mass. Steam plumes out of the burger and the first mouthful takes me back to the diners of my youth. This is my own comfort food, a style that may be foreign and unnatural to many, but one that reminds me of Central Alberta.

Eggs fried over easy and served with biscuits, clubhouse sandwiches, banana cream pie, mushroom burgers with a menu typo that says "fried mush." These are all things I remember from long ago. (Well, maybe not the fried mush.) South Fork has captured those elements on its flat-top grill and in its lumber-lined dining room with no biffies. (They're outside, around back. Don't worry, there's heat, running water and flush toilets.)

South Fork is a throwback to a different era and remains true to those roots. But it also stays current and popular with High River residents and visitors. They serve a chicken quesadilla, spicy fries and even a veggie burger. And for the kids, they do Mickey Mouse pancakes. (Hey, can I get some of those, too?)

Regulars gather to solve the problems of the world, the coffee pot keeps coming around and you should save your fork—there's pie. Even as visitors, we end up spending more time than we planned. It's like going home.

Address
110 – 1 Street W
High River

Phone
403.652.3787

Hours
Monday – Saturday
7 am – 3 pm

Reservations
Accepted

Cards
V, MC, Debit

Drinks
No alcoholic beverages

Takeout
Yes

Outdoor Dining
Deck

Website
No

Spolumbo's

Italian Deli

Sᴘᴏʟᴜᴍʙᴏ's has become so entrenched in Calgary's culture and cuisine that some visitors insist on a trip to the Inglewood sausage house whenever they're in town. (I've had to detour here when taking folks back to the airport.) Golf tournaments wouldn't be allowed to operate without Spolumbo's sausages served on at least one hole. And what would a Stamps game be without a hot sausage? The Spoletini-Palumbo boys have built a meaty little empire, one link at a time.

You can find Spolumbo's products on numerous menus and in most grocery stores around town, but if I'm in the area, I'll pop into their home base to get the freshest chicken-apple sausages (my favourites) possible. It's a plain, pleasant room, sun-washed to the south and busy, busy at lunchtime. The tables are arranged cafeteria style, and sports memorabilia cover the walls.

But my quick drop-in can turn into a serious lunch if I'm not careful. I start out conscientiously enough, avoiding the deli lineup and heading straight to the fresh sausage area. I try to look away from the meatball sandwiches and the shiny, grilled sausages just waiting for someone to claim them. But how can I ignore their sultry enticements?

Before I know it, the scent of sausage has drawn me to the deli line, and it's game on. Sometimes it's the meatballs, sometimes the meat loaf (soooo good) and sometimes the Italian sausage. That's the power of meat, Spolumbo's style.

Address
1308 – 9 Avenue SE

Phone
403.264.6452

Hours
Monday – Saturday
8 am – 5:30 pm

Reservations
Accepted for
private room only

Cards
V, MC, AE, Debit

Drinks
Beer & wine only
No corkage

Takeout
Yes

Outdoor Dining
No

Website
spolumbos.com

Spoonful

I T seems the revitalization of the Bowness Hotel has gone on forever. At least now there are a number of offices and retail outlets in the old building, one of which is Spoonful, a forty-two-seat restaurant that serves both Chinese and Thai food.

Certainly the Chinese side of things is good, at least what I've tried. The couple who run Spoonful hail from Hong Kong, and they do a delicious hot-and-sour soup. It has the right balance of hot (chilies) and sour (vinegar) and loads of fresh bamboo shoots, barbecued pork and tofu. They add a bunch of shrimp and serve it in a cafe au lait bowl for $7.50. It's a big bowl of very good soup.

When they wander into Thai cuisine, though, I think things get a little inauthentic. Not that the food doesn't taste good. It does. But the flavours seem more of a Hong Kong interpretation of Thai cuisine than a true rendition. So the pad Thai noodles come in a tomatoey sauce, as does a dish of Thai chicken noodles. Again, it's tasty, just not like anything I've had in Thailand.

But Spoonful is cheap. Everything is under $14, with lunch combos topping out at $10 and providing more food than can fit neatly on the platter. Yep, your combo comes on a platter—that's how much food you get. Which is a little more than a spoonful.

Address
6404 Bowness Road NW
(Bowness Hotel)

Phone
403.247.4499

Hours
Monday – Thursday
11 am – 9 pm

Friday
11 am – 10 pm

Saturday
4 pm – 10 pm

Sunday
4 pm – 9 pm

Reservations
Accepted

Cards
V, MC, Debit

Drinks
Fully licensed
Corkage $12 per bottle

Takeout
Yes
Delivery

Outdoor Dining
No

Website
No

Sunny | Vietnamese

SUNNY is a great name for this Chinatown Vietnamese restaurant. Being upstairs, they've been able to incorporate a skylight into the place. And they've gone for a huge one that spills sunlight into the light green room, brightening the surroundings.

Sunny offers a fairly short list—by Vietnamese standards—of culinary classics. There are big bowls of different pho noodle soups and bun vermicelli plus various rice plates topped with things like a charbroiled lemon-grass chicken and shredded pork combo ($9). They also have Cambodian clear noodles served either in a mild chicken broth or with the broth on the side (both $8.50).

Looking for more intensity, I tried a satay beef and cha gio bun. That combination is not actually on the menu, but when I asked for it, they were happy to oblige. (Really pleasant, quick service here—that's sunny, too.) The satay sauce was one of the best I've had—thick with ground peanuts, heavy with chilies, a terrific counterpoint to the mild vermicelli noodles. The cha gio spring rolls were likewise excellent, crisp and flavourful. Not as light as some, but not as heavy as most. As for the rest of the bowl, it was a hearty serving of noodles doused with fish sauce. For $9, an excellent lunch.

I also noticed that the pho and rice dishes being delivered around me came with heaping piles of fresh greens. Nice. Especially as they sat glimmering in the sunlight under the skylight at Sunny.

Address
111 – 2 Avenue SE
(Second Floor)

Phone
403.265.2210

Hours
Daily
10:30 am – 4:30 pm

Reservations
Accepted

Cards
V, MC, Debit

Drinks
No alcoholic beverages

Takeout
Yes

Outdoor Dining
No

Website
No

Sushi Haru | Japanese

THERE may be some who think you can't find good sushi, especially at a good price, in Airdrie. Well, I'm happy to say that Sushi Haru is around to prove naysayers wrong.

Sushi Haru occupies a mall bay in typical mall-bay fashion with its rectangular room and sparse decorations. It has a simple look with tables lined up and separated by rice-paper dividers. There's a sushi bar at one end, and the whole place seats about sixty.

Sushi Haru's menu—true to its name—covers a lot of sushi. But there is a list of non-sushi dishes like udon noodles, miso soup, shrimp and vegetable tempura, and deep-fried chicken karaage.

Back to sushi, though. I had the Ninja Combo, which was $20. At most Calgary sushi joints, I can pack away $20 worth in about five minutes. At Sushi Haru, the Ninja is twenty-one pieces (twenty one!) of nigiri sushi, large and small rolls, and sashimi. Each cut of fish is large and clean—this is well prepared. The sashimi cuts would pass for fillets in many places. So I was happy, and it took me longer than five minutes to eat it all. But I also had to order the Airdrie Roll: Crab meat (fake, but that's OK) was wrapped with nori and then wrapped with sushi rice, and it was all topped with broiled, eel-sauced salmon. Eight big pieces for $6. And the sushi rice was as good as I've had anywhere.

So, yes, good sushi in Airdrie. Works for me.

Address
109, 400 Main Street
Airdrie

Phone
403.948.6373

Hours
Tuesday – Sunday
Noon – 2:30 pm

Tuesday – Thursday &
Sunday
5 pm – 9 pm

Friday & Saturday
5 pm – 10 pm

Reservations
Accepted

Cards
V, MC, AE, Debit

Drinks
Beer & sake only
Corkage $5 per bottle

Takeout
Yes
Delivery

Outdoor Dining
No

Website
No

Sushi Hibiki | Japanese

THIS used to be a great little hole in the wall called Cafe de Tokyo—a cold, drafty place with potholes you could lose your orange-vinyl chair in. But the owner, a master soup maker, retired a few years ago and the place became Sushi Hibiki.

The new owners renovated the narrow, twenty-five-seat space as much as they could. The floor is more or less even now, and the room is a lot spiffier. It's still drafty, but what can you do?

In spite of its name, noodle bowls—ramen, udon or soba—are one of the main attractions at Sushi Hibiki. Some are in miso stock, some in pork stock, some in fish broth, some hot, some cold, some topped with tempura prawns or teriyaki chicken, some topped with chopped nori or boiled eggs. All are under $10. And all are served with house-prepared soy sauce. Slurpy, salty goodness in a bowl.

At lunch, another option is a bowl of rice topped with barbecued eel or tempura prawns or chicken teriyaki and sided with miso soup and salad. Or one of the bento boxes, which include some sushi. (Yes, they do sushi at Sushi Hibiki, but it doesn't come cheap.)

I've enjoyed everything I've tried here, even though they don't make their own noodles. They can't do it all—and you have to like a place that does its own soy sauce.

Address
6, 630 – 1 Avenue NE

Phone
403.264.1211

Hours
Tuesday – Saturday
11:30 am – 2 pm
5 pm – 9 pm

Reservations
Accepted for up to 8

Cards
V, MC, AE, Debit

Drinks
Fully licensed
No corkage

Takeout
Yes

Outdoor Dining
No

Website
sushihibiki.com

Taketomi Village

THERE'S an odd yet engaging cross-culturalism about Taketomi Village. The little eatery has a Japanese name but serves Chinese and Indian Hakka-style food. And lively, red Chinese lanterns contrast with the white Japanese rice-paper partitions hanging over the sushi bar. At least, what *used* to be the sushi bar when Taketomi Village was a Japanese restaurant. Confused? That's understandable.

When the current owners took over the space from the Japanese ones a few years ago, they didn't make many physical changes. In fact, they even kept the name and the sign. They introduced a completely new menu, though—one that is not only broadly Chinese, but includes a number of Hakka dishes, too. Indian Hakka is a hybridized cuisine—integrating Indian spices and Chinese cooking techniques—that comes from an enclave of Chinese Hakka people who have lived in India for decades.

Although the Hakka dishes constitute a small portion of the menu here, they make up the majority of the business at Taketomi. Items like the chili beef, curry chicken and Manchurian noodles are wok fried and loaded with perspiration-inducing chilies, while the Hakka seafood soup shows a slightly milder profile. But more sizzle returns with the Szechuan dishes and even a few Thai offerings. It's a long, diverse menu.

One thing you won't find on the menu anymore is pork. Taketomi aims to satisfy all their customers, so the pig is gone and cross-culturalism lives on.

Address
136, 920 – 36 Street NE

Phone
403.207.8608

Hours
Monday – Thursday
Noon – 11 pm

Friday
Noon – midnight

Saturday
1 pm – midnight

Sunday
1 pm – 11 pm

Reservations
Accepted

Cards
V, MC, Debit

Drinks
Fully licensed
No corkage

Takeout
Yes

Outdoor Dining
No

Website
No

Tango Bistro

WHAT do you do when you're one of the oldest restaurants in town (born in 1967) and you want to attract a new and younger crowd? According to Smuggler's Inn, the destination of choice for prime rib in dark surroundings for over forty years, you blow up (figuratively, that is) a dining room and start over.

Now don't worry, all you prime-rib and dark-surroundings fans. You can still get your fix in what remains of Smuggler's. But the west-facing dining room—the one with the windows—is now Tango Bistro, a place that specializes in a "contemporary small plates" menu.

Think pear and Gorgonzola flatbread ($9), pulled pork poutine ($9), pecan-crusted goat cheese ($10) and wild-boar-bacon-wrapped beef tenderloin ($11). Don't expect huge portions—this is small-plates dining, after all. We find about four dishes are good for the two of us, but you can eat light or large. The menu works well for groups, too, because you can satisfy a divergent collection of appetites. From wonton-crusted prawns and gnocchi with pancetta to a lime-cured ceviche and yam fries with chipotle aioli, Tango covers a lot of bases. (Small individual meals are also available for $11 to $15.)

The room itself has been redone in lighter, brighter tones with banquettes and booths and a wine wall near the entrance. (A nice wine list with many bottles $30 to $50.) With its high ceilings and fireplace, it's a comfortable, casual place for a meal. And it makes everything old new again.

Address
6920 Macleod Trail S

Phone
403.252.4365

Hours
Sunday & Monday
4:30 pm – 10 pm

Tuesday – Thursday
11:30 am – 10 pm

Friday & Saturday
11:30 am – midnight

Reservations
Accepted

Cards
V, MC, AE, Debit

Drinks
Fully licensed
Corkage $12.50 per bottle

Takeout
Yes

Outdoor Dining
Yes

Website
tangobistro.com

Taste

SMALL plates are a big trend right now. Unfortunately, some are small in size but not in price. At Taste, though, the price matches the size.

The process here is simple. Everything on the evening menu costs $5, $10, $15 or $20. So you can have some wild mushroom gnocchi with truffle oil ($10) and a tomato salad with basil mascarpone and a balsamic reduction ($10) and stay within our budget. Or some duck-fat drizzled popcorn ($5) and pistachio-crusted lamb chops ($15) or a full cheese board ($20). Deals. If you come for lunch, you'll see a menu of soups, salads, pastas and sandwiches topping out at $12. Things like a grilled sandwich of Brie, blue cheese and aged Cheddar ($12) and a beef dip with Cheddar ($12) are among the offerings. (So, again, the budget works.)

Taste is tiny and keeps it simple. But they don't skimp on quality. Rather, they keep the menu efficient and cost-effective. Same with the wine list. Each month, six red wines and six white ones are selected to pair with the food. Want something else? Too bad. Wait for next month.

The dining room is tight and efficient, too, with four high tables seating six each plus a few smaller tables. So you may end up sitting with other folks and sharing stories. (And your food, too, if you'd like.) Or you can just kick back and enjoy the passing world, one small plate at a time.

Address
1210 – 1 Street SW

Phone
403.233.7730

Hours
Monday – Saturday
11:30 am – midnight

Reservations
Not accepted

Cards
V, MC, AE, Debit

Drinks
Fully licensed
No corkage

Takeout
Lunchtime only

Outdoor Dining
Small patio

Website
taste-restaurant.com

Tazza | Middle Eastern

Ask many Calgarians—especially Bridgelanders—about their favourite Middle Eastern cafe and their eyes will light up, they'll expel a longing sigh and simply say, "Tazza." It's just one of those places that everyone loves.

And for good reason. Owned and operated by the Traya family since 2004, Tazza offers what they call "a fresh taste of the Old World." And fresh it is, with everything made daily and all orders prepared on the spot. Even the name Tazza comes from the Arabic word for freshness.

Tazza's food is zippy enough to please any palate. It jumps with lemon, mint, garlic and fresh herbs—the traditional flavours of the Middle East. The falafel is fabulous, the tabbouleh terrific, the labneh lovely and the shawarma sensational. And, of course, there are options to satisfy vegetarians and carnivores alike. The fatayer alone, a savoury, stuffed pastry, comes in four versions, two of which are vegetarian. You can even get the tabbouleh, usually served as a salad, as a sandwich in a fresh-baked pita.

The Traya's friendly welcome enhances the warmth of the food and the experience. Pop in for a quick shish taouk sandwich to-go and you may be seduced into staying for a chat over a cup of made-to-order Arabic coffee (or a heavenly Angel's espresso) and a honey-drenched dessert. And if the sun is shining on Tazza's patio, you may just linger awhile longer and quickly add Tazza to your favourites, too.

Address
1105 – 1 Avenue NE

Phone
403.263.5922

Hours
Monday – Saturday
10:30 am – 6:30 pm

Reservations
Not accepted

Cards
V, MC, AE, Debit

Drinks
No alcoholic beverages

Takeout
Yes

Outdoor Dining
Patio

Website
tazzafresh.com

Tiffin

TIRED of your usual food places? Looking to take the kids somewhere with entertainment value? Have you tried Tiffin? I mention it for a number of reasons.

First, the food: It's Indian cuisine with an East African influence. So you've got coconut chicken curry, fried cassava in spicy tomato sauce, shish kebabs and chickpea-potato curry. (Yes, butter chicken, too.) The flavours and ingredients are slightly different from our more common Northern Indian restaurants. They use a little less fat here and a little less spice.

Second, the setting: It's a former fast-food joint that's bright and pleasant and indestructible for a quick dine-in.

Third, the tiffins themselves: They're stainless steel stacking containers to transport your food if you take it to-go. You can bring your own tiffins or borrow some (with a deposit) from the folks here. The kids will love all the little pots.

Fourth, the parking: There's lots of it. Right outside the door.

Fifth, the roti machine: It's a big glassed-in machine planted by the ordering counter. Balls of whole wheat dough enter at the top level and make their way along a series of conveyors. They're flattened and then cooked on hot griddles as they move along, flipping every once in a while to cook both sides. On a busy day, Tiffin may make 2,500 roti. It's a hypnotizing machine. Park the kids in front of it and they're occupied until you're ready to leave.

Need I say more?

Address
188 – 28 Street SE
(Plaza 28)

Phone
403.273.2420

Hours
Monday – Thursday
11:30 am – 9 pm

Friday
11:30 am – 11 pm

Saturday
11:30 am – 10 pm

Reservations
Accepted

Cards
V, MC, AE, Debit

Drinks
Beer & wine only
No corkage

Takeout
Yes
Delivery

Outdoor Dining
No

Website
tiffincurry.com

Tommy Burger Bar

Gourmet Burgers

Tommy Burger Bar is an odd duck. It used to be an Arby's, so it has televisions everywhere, and it still has the old drive-through lane onto Macleod Trail. But at the same time, it has stylish chandeliers, serves Kobe beef and lobster Mac and Cheese, and has a cocktail menu. So it's not exactly a hole in the wall.

Tommy is a New Age burger bar, the kind of place where your all-natural Galloway beef burger can be topped with avocado and Camembert or your veggie burger can be gussied up with garlic aioli. (Aioli on a veggie burger? That's pretty la-de-da, ain't it?) But they also serve milkshakes—and darned good ones at that—in tall shake glasses with the metal shake mixer on the side for refills. Now that's class.

Sure, those burgers are around $12.50 and, granted, a shake is $6, but the Jughead sandwiches are a meal in themselves, so they fit in this book. Besides, they come with a choice of fries, salad or soup, too. If burgers aren't your thing, there are salmon or pulled pork sandwiches, Nathan's hot dogs, and the Mac and Cheese. (Which, at $24, *doesn't* fit in this book.)

So if you can rationalize the big bucks for a burger topped with, say, smoked Gouda, an over-easy egg and sautéed mushrooms, Tommy might be your place. Service is good, too—a cross between the old diner style and a good contemporary place.

Address
9629 Macleod Trail S

Phone
403.258.0668

Hours
Monday – Thursday
11 am – 10 pm

Friday – Sunday
11 am – 11 pm

Reservations
Recommended weekends & for large groups

Cards
V, MC, Debit
ATM

Drinks
Fully licensed
No corkage

Takeout
Yes

Outdoor Dining
Patio

Website
tommyburger.ca

Tres Marias | Mexican

BACK when the Calgary Farmers' Market was located in an old airplane hangar on the Currie Barracks, a number of great little businesses sprang up. One of them was Tres Marias, a Mexican food stall that sold their homemade tortillas and salsas and chips and also sold Mexican products like canned chilies, mole and hominy to complement their in-house fare. We used their tortillas on many occasions and perked up a few dinners with their delicious salsas.

When the Market moved to just off Blackfoot Trail, Tres Marias opted to open their own independent shop in Marda Loop instead. At their new place, they have all their own products and the imported goods plus a cooler of things from local producers such as Vital Green Organic Dairy and Valta Bison. And they have enough room left over to wedge in twelve chairs at three tables.

In the back, there's a kitchen making good Mexican meals. You'll find such dishes as tortilla soup and tamales, enchiladas and empanadas, huevos rancheros and quesadillas. Not necessarily all at once. The staff choose a selection to serve each day.

One chilly winter visit, we ordered tortilla soup, a chicken tostada and a Mexican salad. We enjoyed it all, though our favourite was the tostada with its crisp corn tortilla topped with black beans, shredded chicken, sour cream, mozzarella and salsa. We may not have been on a plane south, but at least our taste buds got to head that way.

Address
3514 – 19 Street SW

Phone
403.243.5335

Hours
Monday – Friday
11 am – 7 pm

Saturday
10 am – 3 pm

Reservations
Not accepted

Cards
V, MC, Debit

Drinks
No alcoholic beverages

Takeout
Yes

Outdoor Dining
No

Website
tresmarias.ca

Trung Nguyen

Vietnamese Subs

IN the world of Vietnamese sub sandwiches, there are many that just don't measure up. The meats are dull and cheap, the veggies even duller and cheaper, the sauces lacklustre and the buns soggy or stale. But you won't find any of the above at Trung Nguyen, probably the oldest shop of its kind in the city.

Most often referred to as "that little place across from the Harry Hays Building," Trung Nguyen defines the term "hole in the wall." I've seen larger closets. The seating area consists of just three tables tucked into the hallway in front of the prep area.

But day after day (literally, they almost never close), Trung Nguyen pumps out great sandwiches packed with things like satay or lemon-grass chicken or shredded pork or that unique Calgary ingredient—ginger beef. Whatever you order, it will be loaded into a fine crusty roll and topped with your choice of crunchy vegetables and a hearty smothering of sauce. (Just have veggies if you want—it'll still be delicious.) If you'd like, they'll pass your sub through a conveyor oven to lightly toast it. Before you know it, you'll be enjoying one of the best subs in the city, for just $6 or $7.

Recently, Trung Nguyen expanded into the growing world of bubble teas, too. Loads of folks love the fresh avocado or passion fruit teas swimming with tapioca pearls. As if the subs alone weren't enough to keep you coming back.

Address
10, 132 – 3 Avenue SE

Phone
403.266.0728

Hours
Monday – Friday
10 am – 6 pm

Saturday & Sunday
11 am – 5 pm

Reservations
Not accepted

Cards
Cash only

Drinks
No alcoholic beverages

Takeout
Yes

Outdoor Dining
No

Website
No

Tu Tierra | Mexican

IF you have a copy of my first *Cheap Eats* book, you'll note an entry for Mi Tierra, a little taqueria in Oakridge. It closed in early 2011, but a few years before that, the owners also opened a full-scale restaurant in Acadia called Tu Tierra. This one is still around and seats about sixty in a vibrantly coloured setting that's washed in bright overhead lights. For decades, this spot was a Chinese restaurant, but all evidence of that is gone except for the pagoda-shaped sign outside that is now highlighted by a Mexican chili logo.

Tu Tierra offers a broad menu that includes tacos filled with cochinita pibil (shredded pork in an orange sauce) and enchiladas rolled with chicken and topped with a tomatillo sauce. There's a barbacoa lamb stew, chile rellenos and shrimp ceviche. And if you want a salsa that will blister your lips, they'll serve you that, too. (Don't worry if you like your food mild—there's a wide range of heat here.)

Most mains range between $10 and $15, with tacos starting at $9.49. Even the seafood burrito with scallops, shrimp, basa and crab is only $15.

The food has lively flavours, but can sometimes take awhile to wander its way to your table. Regardless, Tu Tierra has an infectious and loud energy, and after a margarita or two, you'd swear you were in the heart of Mexico.

Address
30, 8316 Fairmount Drive SE

Phone
403.252.5566

Hours
Monday
11 am – 8 pm

Tuesday
11 am – 8:30 pm

Wednesday – Saturday
11 am – 9 pm

Sunday
11 am – 7:30 pm

Reservations
Accepted for groups of 4 or more

Cards
V, MC, Debit

Drinks
Fully licensed
No corkage

Takeout
Yes

Outdoor Dining
No

Website
tutierra.ca

Tubby Dog

CAUTION: If you're concerned about ingredients like Miracle Whip, processed cheese, bacon bits and deep-fried wieners, better flip to another review. But if you just went, "Mmmm—deep-fried wieners," Tubby Dog may be your place. Especially if it's 3 am and you have the munchies.

Since 2005, Tubby Dog has been building some of the most outlandish hot dogs ever. Tried the PBJ Dog covered in peanut butter and jelly? Want to up the ante on that with an indelicate coating of Cap'n Crunch? (That's the Cap'ns Dog.) How about the Sumo, outfitted with Japanese mayo, wasabi, pickled ginger and seaweed? There's always Sherm's Ultimate Gripper, the bacon-wrapped, deep-fried dog laden with a fried egg and a list of other ingredients too long for this page. (Though I will tell you it's covered in homemade chili, which is now also available by the bowl for 5 bucks.)

Team up anything with an order of yam fries or Tubby chips, and a red cafeteria tray covered with wax paper will quickly appear, overflowing with your order. Just try to pound through it. Call in reinforcements if you need to, especially if it's 3:30 in the morning. They'll be happy to hear from you.

Or just sit awhile, sip a beer and enjoy the oddball ambience of Tubby Dog. It's a 17th Avenue classic that is totally non-judgemental and accepting. They even have vegetarian dogs. So come on in, choose your own toppings if you'd like and have a Tubby experience. It's no crime if you can't finish.

Address
103, 1022 – 17 Avenue SW

Phone
403.244.0694

Hours
Sunday – Thursday
11:30 am – 10 pm

Friday & Saturday
11:30 am – 4 am

(Hours may vary seasonally & with weather)

Reservations
Recommended for groups

Cards
Cash only
ATM

Drinks
Fully licensed
Corkage fee available

Takeout
Yes

Outdoor Dining
Big bench

Website
tubbydog.com

Ukrainian Fine Foods

Ukrainian

WHENEVER I step into Ukrainian Fine Foods, I feel like dancing. The smell of cabbage rolls and borscht and the sight of perogies and kolbassa kick-start youthful memories of wedding dances and other celebrations in my Central Alberta homeland. So with a polka playing in my head, I'll order my cabbage roll-perogie-kolbassa combo and settle in for a fine Ukrainian feed.

I love that the smallest combo meal here is a mix of six perogies and a couple of huge chunks of kolbassa for $6.75. And that it ramps up from there to plates of enormity. Yet you won't go over 10 bucks, unless you add on extras. Ukrainian Fine Foods offers some of the best dollar-for-calorie value in this book.

I also love that the borscht is red, meaning that it's made with beets. And that every weekday they have lunch specials—roast pork on Monday, baked ham or spaghetti and meatballs on Tuesday, and so on. (I love that little multicultural slant, too.) And dare I love that there is nothing green on this menu? (Unless you count the cabbage itself, that is.)

OK, moving along, what else do I love? That the same crew who've been rolling and scooping cabbage rolls for years is still at it. And that you can get their food—to eat in or take home—at the Crossroads Market, too.

There's no doubt that Ukrainian food is an acquired taste. I acquired it at a young age, and its aroma alone makes me want to kick up my heels.

Address
540 Cleveland Crescent SE

Phone
403.287.8884

Hours
Monday – Friday
9 am – 3 pm

Reservations
Not accepted

Cards
V, MC, AE, Debit

Drinks
No alcoholic beverages

Takeout
Yes

Outdoor Dining
1 picnic table

Website
No

Other Location

1235 – 26 Avenue SE
(Crossroads Market)
No phone

The Unicorn

"**A** LONG time ago, when the earth was green," there were no pubs in Calgary. So The Irish Rovers, flush from the success of their "Unicorn" song, opened Calgary's first pub in the basement of the Lancaster Building. That was in 1979, and the Old World pub atmosphere of The Unicorn became an instant beacon for those who craved a well-pulled pint in a cozy, subterranean space.

Now, more than three decades later, The Unicorn lives on and is just starting to gain a patina of age. There have been various owners over the years who have respected the original tone and look, so it remains a discreet downtown hideaway. The many televisions are small, and the volume is kept low. The long, oval bar is set off to one side rather than hogging the middle of the room. And the staff are a pleasant hybrid of efficient pubsters and professional downtowners.

The menu combines highlights of the New World and the Old. They do a fine fish and chips, for instance, but they do it with Louisiana catfish. There's a vegetarian ciabatta sandwich and a jerk-turkey burger alongside a ploughman's lunch and a "Black'n'Tan" (stout and pale ale) Mac and Cheese. They even do five different kinds of salads so as to appeal to a broad spectrum of the downtown crowd.

And of course, The Unicorn pulls a pint or two, including the ever popular Guinness.

Address
304 Stephen Avenue SW
(Lower Level)

Phone
403.234.8816

Hours
Monday – Wednesday
11 am – 1 am

Thursday – Saturday
11 am – 2 am

Sunday
Noon – 8 pm

Reservations
Recommended

Cards
V, MC, AE, Debit
ATM

Drinks
Fully licensed
No corkage

Takeout
Yes

Outdoor Dining
Patio

Website
unicorncalgary.com

Urban Rice

LOOKED up Urban Rice's Chinatown address and thought it looked familiar. When I got there, I realized I'd reviewed this spot several times. It's at the base of a condo tower in a space that's housed many restaurants over the years. This one, I'm hoping, will be a keeper.

Urban Rice (I love the name) serves Hong Kong cuisine, meaning largely the Cantonese style you'll find in Hong Kong today. And as well, since Hong Kong draws its flavours from across China, you'll find dishes from regions such as Szechuan and Hunan, too. (Note: You'll find a similar but smaller menu at their Sun Life food court.)

Here in Chinatown, you'll find a collection of dishes such as beef short ribs in a black-pepper sauce, steamed chicken with loads of finely julienned ginger and green onions, and a dish of spinach and eggs. Plus they serve dim sum every day, from opening until 4 pm.

For that egg dish, they scramble up a half-dozen eggs, sauté a big bunch of spinach and combine the two. It works deliciously. So do the beef short ribs, served sticky, peppery and meaty, albeit a little chewy. And that chicken is tender and moist, piqued wonderfully by the ginger and onion.

Servings are huge. Two dishes will feed two people with leftovers. Three will give you at least another meal. Four will help you remember this address for a long time.

Address
108 – 3 Avenue SW
(Five Harvest Plaza)

Phone
403.984.3380

Hours
Daily
8 am – 10 pm

Reservations
Recommended weekends
& for large groups

Cards
V, MC, Debit

Drinks
Beer & wine only
Corkage $5 per bottle

Takeout
Yes
Delivery

Outdoor Dining
No

Website
No

Other Location

112 – 4 Avenue SW
(Sun Life Plaza)
403.461.9108

Valbella Cafe | European Deli

VALBELLA meats show up on many restaurant menus and in many markets around these parts. But a pilgrimage to Canmore's Valbella Gourmet Foods itself is a required activity for those who enjoy the pleasures of cured meats. Valbella is a carnivore's dream—since 1978, a place to indulge in some of the best meats in Western Canada.

Pull into their parking lot and the smell of smoking meats will hit you the moment you open your car door. That's non-subtle marketing, for sure. Enter the deli section, behold the racks of cured sausages and the display cases filled with hams, bacon and the hundreds of other Valbella products, and—sorry vegans—your primal meat-devouring urges may surface.

Fortunately, years ago the Valbella folks had the good sense to open a cafe alongside their deli. This reduces the number of greasy-handed drivers chomping on chimney sticks or chunks of gypsy salami. Instead, anyone with immediate needs can order up a sandwich packed with various cold cuts along with a bowl of soup (perhaps lentil and smoky bacon that day) and relax right there.

So go. Eat. Then shop. Even pick up some fresh meats to toss on the barbecue. (Or if it's almost Christmas or Thanksgiving, place your order for a turducken layered with cranberry-apple stuffing.) Add in some salads and maybe some sweet or savoury pies, a little bread and a few cheeses. Now you're ready for a Valbella extravaganza at home. Just refrain from the salami-handed driving to get there.

Address
104 Elk Run Boulevard
Canmore

Phone
403.678.4109

Hours
Monday – Friday
8 am – 6 pm

Saturday
9 am – 5 pm

Reservations
Not accepted

Cards
V, MC, Debit

Drinks
No alcoholic beverages

Takeout
Yes

Outdoor Dining
2 picnic tables

Website
valbellagourmetfoods.ca

Vendome | Italian Café

BACK when Vendome Café was Heartland Café, it was a funky, creaky-floored place that was always busy. Now that it's Vendome, it seems even busier. How did they do that?

It's not that it looks a lot different than before. Sure, the new owners buffed it up a bit, but the floors still creak and the room continues to exude the lustre befitting a century-old brick building. They mounted chalkboard menus in ornate, gilded frames behind a small open kitchen, and they added an impressive espresso machine to pull locally roasted shots from Paradise Mountain Organic Coffee. And they squeezed as many seats as possible into the room. Mostly, though, they left it alone to tell its own story.

Vendome attracts an all-age crowd, from neighbouring seniors to the baby-stroller brigade. Customers line up to order at the counter, sharing space with the always-moving staff, and then grab a seat when one opens up. They wait for their morning coffee or eggs Benedict (classic, crab or vegetarian) or their panini or vegetarian lasagna.

People seem to like Vendome, and I do too. It has a sense of age and permanence—the warmth of the neighbourhood and the individuality of a small business. There is none of the synthetic feel of a chain joint here—just good food, good coffee, good folks, good times. And creaky floors.

Address
940 – 2 Avenue NW

Phone
403.453.1140

Hours
Monday – Friday
7 am – 6 pm

Saturday & Sunday
8 am – 5 pm

Reservations
Not accepted

Cards
V, MC, AE, Debit

Drinks
No alcoholic beverages

Takeout
Yes

Outdoor Dining
4 benches

Website
vendomecafe.com

Vienna Lux

Hungarian & Austrian

THE first time I saw Vienna Lux' chicken schnitzel sandwich, I uttered an expletive not fit for this book. I had been expecting a bun filled with a nice piece of schnitzelled (flattened, breaded, fried) chicken topped with roasted peppers and sauerkraut. But what I got was about three times that. Literally.

Three—yup, three—layers of schnitzel were loaded into a huge Kaiser bun and smothered in sautéed peppers and sauerkraut. Even cut in half, each half was almost too big to hold. On my first try, I only ate a quarter of the sandwich. (That's right. Me. I only ate a quarter.) But it was so good. I considered calling my golf buddies to take on the rest, but thought better of it and saved it for later. And for only $9? What a bargain.

Vienna Lux makes a variety of Hungarian and Austrian dishes—mostly as sandwiches—in their tidy, orange and red cafe downtown. There's the pork schnitzel sandwich and a fried eggplant one, as well as the chicken schnitzel and a true Wiener schnitzel made with veal. Toppings—cheese, sautéed mushrooms, red cabbage, sauerkraut, roasted sweet peppers, sautéed onions, hot peppers and pickles—are optional. (The mushrooms, cheese and sweet peppers are a buck each; the others are complimentary.)

You might also find a plate of chicken paprikash and some poppyseed muffins as daily specials. And you'll always find a hearty bowl of goulash soup.

So go, be amazed and watch your language.

Address
821 – 4 Avenue SW

Phone
403.452.3737

Hours
Monday – Friday
11 am – 3 pm

Reservations
Accepted

Cards
V, MC, Debit

Drinks
Beer only
No corkage

Takeout
Yes

Outdoor Dining
Patio

Website
viennalux.ca

Village Pita

BACK in the 1980s, a friend of mine would take me to Village Pita for a zataar, a hot pita covered in a coating of thyme, oregano, sumac and sesame seeds. (It was his way of paying me back for all the lunches he'd mooched off me. The zataars were about $2 at the time.) I'm pretty sure I complained to him about his cheapness, but I know I never did about his choice in lunch spots. The zaatar sang with an herbal intensity.

Village Pita moved in the mid-1990s to Short Pants Plaza and still pumps out zataar after zataar, along with falafel—and other—sandwiches and their latest creation, the chicken pocket. They pack cooked chicken, along with pickles, sauce and fresh vegetables, onto a round of fresh dough. The dough is folded over calzone/empanada style, and the pocket is then baked in a conveyor-belt oven. The result is hot, fresh and drippy. The falafel sandwich, rolled in pita (that would be their own Village Pita pita, by the way), is always a winner, too.

And if you'd like to debate the fate of the Flames or Stamps, just join the gaggle of sandwich noshers gathered at the dozen stools along the front window. Enjoy your sandwich and the discussion and then pick up a few Middle Eastern groceries from the store side of Village Pita.

Next time, bring a friend along and treat them to lunch. They'll be happy you did.

Address
255 – 28 Street SE
(Short Pants Plaza)

Phone
403.273.0330

Hours
Monday – Saturday
8 am – 7 pm

Sunday
9 am – 5 pm

Reservations
Not accepted

Cards
Debit
ATM

Drinks
No alcoholic beverages

Takeout
Yes

Outdoor Dining
No

Website
No

Vue | Contemporary Cafe

VUE Cafe is the only eatery in this book that's in an art gallery—guaranteed. The Virginia Christopher Fine Art Gallery, to be exact.

Run by Dwayne and Alberta Ennest of Cuisine Concepts (think Diner Deluxe, Open Range, Big Fish and Urban Baker), Vue is largely a curved dining bar facing into an open kitchen and surrounded by art. You perch on one of twenty chairs and watch the chefs cook lunch, or you can rent the space for an evening function.

It would be easy for such a small and contained place to do a short list of mediocre food. But Vue takes a radical tack: The focus is on local, organic ingredients, intelligently prepared. There's a spinach salad in a honey vinaigrette tossed with candied pecans, roasted apples and aged Cheddar. And a flatbread baked with duck confit, pears, Cambozola cheese and toasted pine nuts. Plus a panini stacked with smoked turkey, arugula and Sylvan Star Gouda and a lamb burger topped with Oka cheese, crabapple jelly and rosemary pesto.

Sound a little fancy for this book? The top price is $15—that's for the lamb burger. Vue offers just exceptional value, especially considering the quality of the ingredients. And the made-just-for-you tone of the place.

Speaking of which, while the made-just-for-you thing is happening, take a look at the art. Nothing like a little edification along with your lunch.

Address
816 – 11 Avenue SW
(Virginia Christopher
Fine Art Gallery)

Phone
403.263.4346

Hours
Tuesday – Saturday
11 am – 4 pm

Reservations
Recommended

Cards
V, AE, MC, Debit

Drinks
Fully licensed
No corkage

Takeout
Yes

Outdoor Dining
No

Website
vuecafe.com

More Bakeries

THERE's been an explosion of bakeries lately and with that has come a wealth of tasty new goodies. Not all of them are cheap, but they're worth checking out. Here are a few I've enjoyed lately.

Empanada Queen

Chilean empanadas—chicken, beef, vegetarian—are a treat at the appropriately named Empanada Queen. (Besides those, there are other savoury items like the shepherd's-pie-styled pastel de choclo.)

4100 Marlborough Drive NE
403.235.0686
empanadaqueen.ca

Itza Bakeshop

Alexandra Chan bakes sinfully divine croissants, pains au chocolat, daily treats and luscious cakes at Itza. (Get it? *It's a bakeshop.*)

908 – 17 Avenue SW
(Devenish Building)
403.228.0044
itzabakeshop.com

Jelly

Grayson Sherman has created a list of hefty, decadent, delectable doughnuts (think PB&J, marshmallow or maple-bacon). My vote for Best New Concept of 2011.

100, 1414 – 8 Street SW
403.453.2053
jellymoderndoughnuts.com

La Creperie

Just look for the lineup waiting for a crepe, croissant, cake or other fine French pastry at this market kiosk. (They've expanded into soup and sandwiches, too.)

7711 Macleod Trail S
(Kingsland Farmers' Market)
403.454.3716

Prairie Mill

House-ground flour is turned into big loaves of tasty bread at this northwest bakery.

4820 Northland Drive NW
(Northland Plaza)
403.282.6455
prairiemillbread.com

Sidewalk Citizen

You'll find Aviv Fried's scones and sourdough breads at many locations around Calgary or you can pick up goodies at his bakery on Fridays and Saturdays, 10 am to 2 pm (or other times, too, but then call ahead to ensure they're open).

5524 – 1A Street SW
403.400.3067
sidewalkcitizenbakery.com

Sweet Provocateur

Kira Desmond brings her avant-garde patisserie to the Kingsland Market in the form of cakes, cookies, confections and other sweet provocations. She's opened Sweet P's Kitchen on 26th Street SE, too, with more sweet treats, plus pizzas, salads and sandwiches.

7711 Macleod Trail S
(Kingsland Farmers' Market)
403.818.7620

4024 – 26 Street SE
403.818.7620

sweetprovocateur.com

Wild Flour

Load up on big loaves of fresh bread, or dine in on granola or soups and thick sandwiches at this busy Banff bakery.

211 Bear Street
(The Bison Courtyard)
Banff
403.760.5074
wildflourbakery.ca

Wilde Grainz

Karen Schoenrank and Teddi Smith bake outstanding artisanal pastries and breads, including their unique Inglewood sourdough.

1218 – 9 Avenue SE
403.767.9006
wildegrainz.com

Yann Haute Patisserie

Macarons are the big thing here, but the talented Yann Blanchard creates a wealth of other gourmet baking, too. And grab a tea or coffee to-go from Tea Urbana in here as well.

329 – 23 Avenue SW
403.244.8091
yannboutique.com

Yum

Variety, quality and service are key at Yum, a Calgary Farmers' Market mainstay. Try the scones and the fine baguette.

510 – 77 Avenue SE
(Calgary Farmers' Market)
403.472.1296
yum-bakery.com

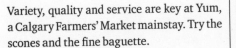

More Buffets

WHAT's quicker and easier than a buffet? There are a few elsewhere in this book, but I thought I'd share more good ones here. At any of the places below, you can order off the menu, too, but then you'd probably be breaking the budget. And you wouldn't have the thrill of going from your car to chowing down in less than three minutes.

Delhi Darbar | Indian (Northern)

At their lunch and dinner buffets, Delhi Darbar mixes contemporary dishes like the dal masoor (yellow lentils in a cumin-scented sauce) with traditional ones like the "railway" mutton curry of lamb and potatoes.

122 – 16 Avenue NE
403.230.3088
Lunch: Sunday – Friday, $12.95
Dinner: Monday – Wednesday, $18.95
delhidarbar.info

Green Chili | Indian (Northern)

At Green Chili's flagship 17th Avenue location, the buffet is packed with intense Northern Indian selections and excellent breads.

1434 – 17 Avenue SW
403.277.3000
Lunch: Sunday – Friday, $13.95
greenchili.ca

Leo Fu's | Chinese

They set out highlights from their regular menu on this buffet and kick it up a notch with extra seafood dishes on Fridays.

511 – 70 Avenue SW
403.255.2528
Lunch: Monday – Thursday, $8.50, Friday, $8.95

Marathon | Ethiopian

Scoop up Ethiopian stews of cabbage and carrot or chicken with ginger and berbere (chili) sauce using the thick, crepey injera bread.

130 – 10 Street NW
403.283.6796
Lunch: Monday – Friday, $12.99
marathonethiopian.com

Rose Garden | Thai

Downtown's most popular Thai buffet continues to attract a huge crowd for the delicate salad rolls and the richly spiced Thai curries.

112 Stephen Avenue SW
(Second Floor)
403.264.1988
Lunch: Monday – Friday,
$15.95

Ruan Thai | Thai

The compact buffet jumps with flavourful Thai dishes in this long-time Beltline restaurant.

101, 1324 – 11 Avenue SW
403.262.7066
Lunch: Monday – Friday,
$13.25
ruanthai.ca

Thai Nongkhai | Thai

Pad Thai noodles, shrimp in green-curry sauce and tom yum soup appear on this once-weekly buffet of fine Thai food.

10, 7400 Macleod Trail S
403.705.3329
Lunch: Tuesday,
$15.95
thai-nk.com

Thai Place | Thai

The buffet is both fragrantly savoury and beautifully presented at the Quality Inn University in Motel Village. Sit by the pool for a tropical feel.

2359 Banff Trail NW
403.338.4405
Lunch: Thursday – Friday,
$12.95

More Coffee (and Tea, too)

CALGARY is a fully caffeinated city, with coffee (and tea) shops percolating into existence frequently. Many are reviewed for their food in this book, but here are a few more stops where you can catch a great buzz—and not just from the caffeine. Most of these places serve some good food, too. (If the ones described below aren't enough to keep your buzz going, try Caffè Artigiano, Chiasso Coffee, Insomnia Coffee Company, The Naked Leaf, Nine Cafe, Oolong Tea House and Steeps.)

Beamers

Both Beamers brew custom-roasted blends for Canmorians looking to kick back or kick off a journey into the wilds.

737 – 7 Avenue
Canmore
403.609.0111

1702 Bow Valley Trail
Canmore
403.678.3988

beamerscoffeebar.ca

Bluerock Cafe

Virginia Ronald pulls Ethical Bean caffeine through her big Elektra espresso machine. Grab a cinnamon bun and an espresso and then stroll the streets of this Foothills town.

94 Elizabeth Street
Okotoks
403.938.3003

Caffe Crema

Caffe Crema attracts a wide range of south-westerners for community events like moms' get-togethers or philosophy chats or acoustic music evenings coupled with rich espressos pulled through a Fratello Slayer machine.

2525 Bridlecrest Way SW
403.457.4022
cremacalgary.com

Caffe Rosso

Tucked into an out-of-the-way location in Ramsay, this Rosso is nonetheless a busy little place. The downtown Convention Centre one is a little easier to find (but parking's harder).

803 – 24 Avenue SE
(Ramsay Exchange)
403.971.1800

140 Stephen Avenue SE
(Telus Convention Centre)
403.264.7900

cafferosso.ca

Central Blends

A fine place for a muffin and always-changing art, Central Blends looks the part of a 1960s coffee house. The brew is good here, too.

203 – 19 Street NW
403.670.5665

DeVille

There are two stylish DeVille cafes featuring high-tech espresso machines and fancy desserts. The Art Central location offers a great view of The Bow building while the Fashion Central one offers a gander of downtown's passing crowds.

100 – 7 Avenue SW
(Art Central)
403.452.7777

807 – 1 Street SW
(Fashion Central)
403.263.0884

devillecoffee.ca

Fratello Analog Café

Coffee roaster Fratello has gone retail with the stylish Analog Café at the Calgary Farmers' Market. Enjoy a pristine cup of individually brewed coffee or an espresso from their custom-built Slayer espresso machine. They do loose tea, too.

510 – 77 Avenue SE
(Calgary Farmers' Market)
No phone
fratellocoffee.com

Heartland Cafe

A meeting place for Bridgelanders, Heartland is a hybrid of sleek modernism and homey rusticity, appropriate for the rebirth of this historic area.

825 – 1 Avenue NE
403.263.4567

Java Jamboree

One of the best and most committed coffee houses for miles around, Java Jamboree caffeinates Cochrane with 49th Parallel beans plus "guest" espressos from other select roasters.

312 – 5 Avenue W
(Cochrane Towne Square)
Cochrane
403.932.6240
javajamboree.ca

A Ladybug

Folks in the southwest community of Aspen Woods line up for their favourite Ladybug pastry and pair it with a Malabar Gold or JJ Bean espresso pulled from a state-of-the-art La Marzocco Strada machine.

10 Aspen Stone Boulevard SW
403.249.5530

Purple Perk

A laptop haven in Mission, Purple Perk pulls locally roasted Big Mountain coffee, serves big slabs of sweets and offers free Wi-Fi.

2212 – 4 Street SW
403.244.1300
purpleperk.com

The Roasterie

A Kensington classic, The Roasterie has been roasting coffee for decades. Tenth Street wouldn't be the same without the scent of their coffee and the sight of coffee hounds clustered out front.

314 – 10 Street NW
403.270.3304

Tea Urbana

Brewing fine teas and coffees to-go, Urbana shares a space with Yann's fabulous croissants and pains au chocolat. They make a fine pairing.

329 – 23 Avenue SW
(inside Yann Haute Patisserie)
Phone TBA
teaurbana.ca

TotaliTea

Over 180 teas—including custom blends—plus scads of tea paraphernalia are available from either location. Pop by for a cuppa, too.

510 – 77 Avenue SE
(Calgary Farmers' Market)
403.668.1426

315 Stephen Avenue SW
(+30 Level, Bankers Hall)
403.266.6567

totalitea.com

More Markets

THESE entries include places to buy ingredients or prepared foods to take home (and sometimes to eat there). Some are large with multiple vendors, while others are small specialists. Though not all are cheap, all offer great products.

BBQ Express

This tiny shop offers excellent Chinese barbecued pork, duck and chicken. Line up, place your order and watch them deftly chop the meats into edible chunks. Enjoy!

1403 Centre Street N
403.230.8888

Calgary Farmers' Market

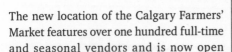

The new location of the Calgary Farmers' Market features over one hundred full-time and seasonal vendors and is now open Thursday through Sunday.

510 – 77 Avenue SE
403.240.9113
calgaryfarmersmarket.ca

Crossroads Market

From Chongo's Market and the Ukrainian Bakery to Old Munich Sausage House and Simple Simon Pies, Crossroads brings a multicultural culinary focus to customers. It's open Friday through Sunday.

1235 – 26 Avenue SE
403.291.5208
crossroadsmarket.ca

Feast Artisan Grocer

Local, artisanal cheeses and charcuterie, hard-to-find ingredients, meals-to-go vacuum packed for reheating and boxed lunches for the trail are all available at this Banff deli.

208 Bear Street
Banff
403.762.2203

Kingsland Farmers' Market

The new market on Macleod Trail showcases dairy, produce and meats, delightful bakeries and artisans of all stripes. It's open Thursday through Sunday.

7711 Macleod Trail S
403.255.3276
kingslandfarmersmarket.com

Las Tortillas

Corn tortillas are pressed, baked and sold here. If you have a few minutes, they can fill some with pork or beef and other good things, too, for a good taco feed.

4100 Marlborough Drive NE
403.273.3555
lastortillasinc.com

L'Epicerie

Luscious French fare—cheeses, rillettes, olive oil—flows from this tiny Beltline deli and eatery. And a new outlet called Le Petit Mousse—part sandwich shop, part creperie and part housewares market—plants a tiny corner of France in the new Calgary Farmers' Market. In either place, the food is as authentic as it gets this side of Brittany.

1325 – 1 Street SE
403.514.0555
dominiquemoussu.com

510 – 77 Avenue SE
(Calgary Farmers' Market)
403.668.1744
lepetitmousse.ca

Salsita

Fresh tomatillos and poblanos, canned chipotles and nopales, dried oregano and guajillos chilies, and house-made salsas are just a few of the things available at this Mexican market.

777 Northmount Drive NW
403.289.2202
salsita.ca

Sunnyside Natural Market

Day in and day out, Sunnyside supports local producers and carries all the natural products you need to make tasty—and healthy—meals at home.

10, 338 – 10 Street NW
403.270.7477
sunnysidemarket.ca

The Lists

THESE lists will guide you to various geographic areas and food styles. Most eateries are arranged alphabetically in the book. When they are not, The Lists below will direct you with one of three types of *see/see also* references: Either you will be directed to another eatery that is, in fact, in alphabetical order in the main body of the book; to another category in The Lists; or to More Bakeries on pages 122 to 123, More Buffets on pages 124 to 125, More Coffee (and Tea, too) on pages 126 to 128, or More Markets on pages 129 to 130.

All establishments are in Calgary unless noted otherwise.

Northeast Calgary

Air Side Bistro
Alberta King of Subs
Bon Appetit
Boogie's Burgers
Byblos Deli
Clay Oven
Delhi Darbar (*see* More Buffets)
Diner Deluxe
Empanada Queen (*see* More Bakeries)
Fat Kee
Heartland Cafe (*see* More Coffee/Tea)
Italian Store, The
Joycee's
Kabab Hut
King's
La Cantina
Las Tortillas (*see* More Markets)
Lina's
Main Dish, The
Mirch Masala
Overeasy Breakfast
Rock, The
Ruby's Kitchen
Sushi Hibiki
Taketomi Village
Tazza

Northwest Calgary

BBQ Express (*see* More Markets)
Bistro Alma
Cadence
Central Blends (*see* More Coffee/Tea)
Chicken on the Way
Dairy Lane
F.A.T.S.
Istanbul
Jimmy's A & A
Kaffee Stube
Kinjo
Kol3
Lazy Loaf & Kettle
Lighthouse Cafe
Marathon (*see* More Buffets)
Peppino
Prairie Mill (*see* More Bakeries)
Roasterie, The (*see* More Coffee/Tea)
Salsita (*see* More Markets)
Spoonful
Sunnyside Natural Market (*see* More Markets)
Thai Place (*see* More Buffets)
Vendome

Southeast Calgary

Babylon
Blackfoot Diner
Caffe Rosso (*see* More
    Coffee/Tea)
Calgary Farmers' Market (*see*
    More Markets)
Crossroads Market (*see* More
    Markets)
eat! eat! in Inglewood
Fire Kirin
Fratello Analog Café (*see* More
    Coffee/Tea)
Fresh Delicious
Holy Smoke
L'Epicerie (*see* More Markets)
Le Petit Mousse (*see* L'Epicerie
    in More Markets)
Lloyd's Patty Plus
Magic Bowl
Main Dish, The
Nem Delight
Pho Binh Minh
Pies Plus
Rocky's Burgers
Saigon Gourmet
Spolumbo's
Sweet P's Kitchen (*see* Sweet
    Provocateur in More
    Bakeries)
Tiffin
TotaliTea (*see* More
    Coffee/Tea)
Tu Tierra
Ukrainian Fine Foods
Village Pita
Wilde Grainz (*see* More
    Bakeries)
Yum (*see* More Bakeries)

Southwest Calgary

Belmont Diner (*see* Galaxie
    Diner)
British Chippy, The
Caffe Crema (*see* More
    Coffee/Tea)
Cowtown Beef Shack
Flat Crepe & Cafe, The
Heritage Deli
Himalayan, The
Kaffir Lime
Kingsland Farmers' Market
    (*see* More Markets)
Kinjo
La Creperie (*see* More
    Bakeries)
Ladybug, A (*see* More
    Coffee/Tea)
Leo Fu's (*see* More Buffets)
Little Chef
Little Lebanon
Loop, The
Momo Sushi
Odyssey
Pâtisserie du Soleil
Pfanntastic Pannenkoek
Phil & Sebastian
Rustic Sourdough Deli
Schooner's
Sidewalk Citizen (*see* More
    Bakeries)
Sweet Provocateur (*see* More
    Bakeries)
Tango Bistro
Thai Nongkhai (*see* More
    Buffets)
Tommy Burger Bar
Tres Marias

Beltline/Mission

Aida's
Big Cheese, The
Boxwood
Bumpy's
Caffè Beano
Caffè Mauro
Famoso
Fat City Franks
Flatlands
Galaxie Diner
Giuseppe's
Green Chili (*see* More Buffets)
Holy Grill
Itza Bakeshop (*see* More Bakeries)
Jelly (*see* More Bakeries)
Kawa
Lion's Den
Mirchi
Mission Diner
Myhre's Deli
Purple Perk (*see* More Coffee/Tea)
Red's Diner
Ruan Thai (*see* More Buffets)
Rustic Sourdough Deli
St. James Corner
Taste
Tea Urbana (*see* More Coffee/Tea)
Tubby Dog
Vue
Yann Haute Patisserie (*see* More Bakeries)

Downtown Calgary

Banh Mi Thi Thi
Caffè Rosso (*see* More Coffee/Tea)
Cultural Centre
DeVille (*see* More Coffee/Tea)
Falafel King
Fresh Delicious
Han's
Jonas' Restaurant
Luxor
Mirchi
Raj Palace
Rose Garden (*see* More Buffets)
Sunny
TotaliTea (*see* More Coffee/Tea)
Trung Nguyen
Unicorn, The
Urban Rice
Vienna Lux

Banff

Barpa Bill's
Feast Artisan Grocer (*see* More Markets)
Owl St. Kitchen
Pad Thai
Wild Flour (*see* More Bakeries)

Canmore

Beamers (*see* More Coffee/Tea)
Communitea
Harvest
La Belle Patate
Railway
Thai Pagoda (*see* Pad Thai)
Valbella Cafe

Foothills/Beyond

Bluerock Cafe (Okotoks, *see* More Coffee/Tea)
Chuckwagon (Turner Valley)
Graduate Foods (Black Diamond)
High Country Cafe (Millarville)
Java Jamboree (Cochrane, *see* More Coffee/Tea)
South Fork (High River)
Sushi Haru (Airdrie)

Austrian/German Hungarian/Swiss

Jonas' Restaurant
Kaffee Stube
Railway (Canmore)
Valbella Cafe (Canmore)
Vienna Lux

Bakeries
(*see also* More Bakeries, pp. 122 – 123)

Byblos Deli
Heritage Deli
Ladybug, A (*see* More Coffee/Tea)
Lazy Loaf & Kettle
Pâtisserie du Soleil
Pies Plus
Rustic Sourdough Deli
Village Pita

Breakfast/Brunch
(*see also* Diners, p. 136)

Bon Appetit
Bumpy's
Cadence
Chuckwagon (Turner Valley)
Communitea (Canmore)
eat! eat! in Inglewood
Flatlands
High Country Cafe (Millarville)
Little Chef
Loop, The
Overeasy Breakfast
Pfanntastic Pannenkoek
Vendome

Buffets
(*see also* More Buffets, pp. 124 – 125)

Clay Oven
Cultural Centre
Himalayan, The
Mirchi (2nd Avenue SW location)
Raj Palace

Burgers/Dogs

Boogie's Burgers
Fat City Franks
Holy Grill
Rocky's Burgers
Tommy Burger Bar
Tubby Dog

Canadian

Alberta King of Subs
Big Cheese, The
Bon Appetit
Boogie's Burgers
Boxwood
Chuckwagon (Turner Valley)
Dairy Lane
eat! eat! in Inglewood
Flatlands
Galaxie Diner
Harvest (Canmore)
High Country Cafe
    (Millarville)
La Belle Patate (Canmore)
Lazy Loaf & Kettle
Little Chef
Myhre's Deli
Owl St. Kitchen (Banff)
South Fork (High River)

Caribbean

Joycee's
Lloyd's Patty Plus

Chinese

Cultural Centre
Fat Kee
Han's
King's
Leo Fu's (see More Buffets)
Magic Bowl
Spoonful
Taketomi Village
Urban Rice

Coffee/Tea
(*see also* More Coffee/Tea,
pp. 126 – 128)

Bumpy's
Cadence
Caffè Beano
Communitea (Canmore)
Kawa
Phil & Sebastian

Contemporary

Bistro Alma
Boxwood
Fire Kirin
Fresh Delicious
Main Dish, The
Tango Bistro
Taste
Vue

Delis/Markets
(*see also* More Markets,
pp. 129 – 130)

Feast (Banff)
Fresh Delicious
Heritage Deli
Italian Store, The
Joycee's
Kaffee Stube
Lina's
Luxor
Main Dish, The
Peppino
Railway (Canmore)
Valbella Cafe (Canmore)

Diners

(see also Breakfast/Brunch, p. 134)

Belmont Diner (see Galaxie Diner)
Blackfoot Diner
Dairy Lane
Diner Deluxe
Galaxie Diner
Lion's Den
Mission Diner
Red's Diner
South Fork (High River)

Fishy

British Chippy, The
Kinjo
Lighthouse Cafe
Momo Sushi
Sushi Haru (Airdrie)
Sushi Hibiki

Indian/Pakistani

Clay Oven
Delhi Darbar (see More Buffets)
Graduate Foods (Black Diamond)
Green Chili (see More Buffets)
Kabab Hut
Mirch Masala
Mirchi
Raj Palace
Ruby's Kitchen
Taketomi Village
Tiffin

Italian/Pizza

Caffè Mauro
Famoso
Giuseppe's
Italian Store, The
La Cantina
Lina's
Peppino
Spolumbo's

Japanese

Kinjo
Momo Sushi
Sushi Haru (Airdrie)
Sushi Hibiki

Latin American

Empanada Queen (see More Bakeries)
Las Tortillas (see More Markets)
Tres Marias
Tu Tierra

Meaty

(see also Burgers/Dogs, p. 134)

Alberta King of Subs
Barpa Bill's (Banff)
Chicken on the Way
Cowtown Beef Shack
Holy Smoke
Myhre's Deli
Odyssey
Railway (Canmore)
Rocky's Burgers
Spolumbo's

Valbella Cafe (Canmore)
Vienna Lux

Middle Eastern

Aida's
Babylon
Byblos Deli
Falafel King
Istanbul
Jimmy's A & A
Little Lebanon
Luxor
Tazza
Village Pita

One of a Kind (Almost)

Air Side Bistro (Casual
    Continental)
Barpa Bill's (Banff, Greek)
Chicken on the Way (Fried
    Chicken)
Fire Kirin (Asian Fusion)
Flat Crepe & Cafe, The
    (Crepes)
Himalayan, The (Nepalese)
Kaffir Lime (Indonesian)
Marathon (Ethiopian, see More
    Buffets)
Pfanntastic Pannenkoek
    (Dutch Pancakes)
Pies Plus (Pies)
Rock, The (Fusion)

Polish/Ukrainian

Heritage Deli
Ukrainian Fine Foods

Pubs

F.A.T.S.
St. James Corner
Schooner's
Unicorn, The

Thai

Pad Thai (Banff)
Rose Garden (see More Buffets)
Ruan Thai (see More Buffets)
Spoonful
Thai Nongkhai (see More
    Buffets)
Thai Pagoda (Canmore, see
    Pad Thai)

Vegetarian

Aida's
Clay Oven
Falafel King
Graduate Foods (Black
    Diamond)
Himalayan, The
Luxor
Marathon (see More Buffets)
Mirchi
Raj Palace
Tazza
Tiffin

Vietnamese

Banh Mi Thi Thi
Kol3
Nem Delight
Saigon Gourmet
Sunny
Trung Nguyen

My Cheapest 13	My Favourite 22
Banh Mi Thi Thi	Aida's
Bon Appetit	Barpa Bill's (Banff)
Falafel King	Caffè Mauro
Fat Kee	Clay Oven
Han's	Flatlands
Heritage Deli	Holy Grill
Little Lebanon	Istanbul
Pho Binh Minh	Jonas' Restaurant
Rustic Sourdough Deli	Kinjo
Trung Nguyen	Lion's Den
Ukrainian Fine Foods	Marathon (*see* More Buffets)
Vienna Lux	Nem Delight
Village Pita	Odyssey
	Owl St. Kitchen (Banff)
	Pâtisserie du Soleil
	Pfanntastic Pannenkoek
	Rocky's Burgers
	Spolumbo's
	Tango Bistro
	Tazza
	Trung Nguyen
	Vue

Late-breaking news...

If anyone can mess with pizza, it's Chef Mario. The day before this book went to press, I happened upon the new **Pimento's Pizzeria** at 814 – 1 Avenue NE (**pimentos.ca**, no phone) where Mario Spina is tossing his always-popular flat-crust pizzas. But he's now kicked it up a notch with a couple of imported high-tech Italian machines that press his pizza dough into flowers and cones. Go. See. The toppings are traditional or creative (how does apricot, Brie and prosciutto sound?). He does dessert pizza cones, too!